First-Grade Diary

Robert Hightower
Lore Rasmussen

The Miquon School
Miquon, Pennsylvania

Rainbow Resources, LLP

Published by Rainbow Resources, LLP
655 Township Road 500E
Toulon, IL 61483
e-mail: info@rainbowresource.com
Phone: 888-841-3456

ISBN 978-1-933407-10-4
10 9 8 7 6 5 4 3   15

Contents

Introduction

The *First-Grade Diary* is a daily log of the progress of a group of 20 primary-grade children in the mathematics laboratory in 1960–61. Most of the children in this class had participated in a readiness program in kindergarten, where they had many free-play sessions with Cuisenaire® rods and other concrete materials. Often they were able to grasp concepts more rapidly and easily than is usual for first-graders and were free to move ahead to new concepts and activities.

The *Diary* was originally kept as a cumulative case history of a specific class to refine methods and procedures for the benefit of future classes. It records games, materials, sequences of developmental activities, and children's responses and insights into mathematical concepts. The learning experiences of these children throughout the school year, their successes and their failures, are described here as an example of one approach to teaching mathematics to a group of first-graders. The children's rapid progress, enthusiasm, and independence indicated that these classroom notes might be of interest and help to others.

Entries for the first part of the school year (September through January) are detailed accounts of the actual daily work of the children. They include diagrams of a variety of concrete materials and teaching aids, specific references to Cuisenaire® rods and to some of the lab sheets as they were used in the activities of the first-grade class. Many of the group activities were recorded in dialogue form so that the responses of the children—even their errors—might illustrate their thinking in the process of discovering certain mathematical concepts. In addition to the actual descriptive class notes, records of work with individual children and evaluations of pupil progress are included.

By the end of January, the children spent most of their time working independently on written materials. The class notes for February through June have been brought together under topics so that instruction for any particular subject can be pursued as far as children require.

The *Diary* is not intended to serve as a manual in the traditional sense, and the teacher is cautioned against following it as a daily guide. It is hoped that teachers will be inspired to develop their own methods of presenting the materials. Since no two groups of children are exactly alike and no two teachers are exactly alike in their style and technique, no two first-grade classes should be expected to follow the same path in learning mathematics.

Teachers who have used the *Diary* report that it has served as a ready source of stimulating ideas. Many of those who teach grades higher than the first have found useful ideas for remedial and review work. We hope that teachers will be inspired to build on this diary, to keep diaries of their own, and to develop their own personal approaches to the Mathematics Laboratory Materials.

September

Summary of Topics

Order
Inequalities
Establishing unit
Building rod patterns
Counting
Numeral recognition
Recognizing number groups
Ordering numbers
One-to-one correspondence
Tallying
Arithmetic operations
Fractions
Geometric recognition

Work with Cuisenaire® rods

I
Free play with rods (10 minutes)

Piles of assorted rods were placed on each table. The children were free to build with the rods. (The majority of the children had attended the kindergarten at Miquon School and had been exposed to the Cuisenaire® rods previously.)

1 Four boys built a "water plant," a "piping system," and an "oil refinery." Other children built pyramids, flat patterns and designs, houses, and boats.

2 Free play ended with a trip around the room to inspect each other's buildings.

II
Group activity:
Discovering one-to-one correspondence

A pile of assorted rods was placed on each table.

1 Lore picked a yellow demonstration rod and held it up in front of the class. The children responded by each picking a yellow rod from his collection of rods. Then Lore held up a red demonstration rod and the children held up a red rod. This procedure continued until the one-to-one correspondence between the demonstration rods and Cuisenaire® rods was established. (The demonstration rods are homemade and cut on an inch scale, while the Cuisenaire® rods are cut on a centimeter scale.)

3

2 Lore picked a white demonstration rod and gave the following direction: Start with the white rod and build a color stairs.

The children built color stairs with Cuisenaire® rods. (Only two children had "gaps" in their stairs.)

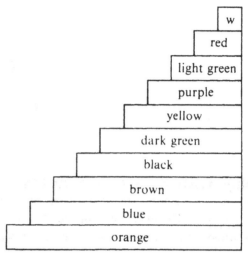

The color stairs

III
Game: "Half of"

Children entering first grade seem to understand the concept of *half*. This probably stems from early experience in sharing with other children—breaking a cookie "in half" (two equal or nearly equal pieces).

1 Lore: Find the rod that is "half of" the purple rod. Find "half of" the red rod. Find "half of" the dark green rod. Find "half of" the orange rod.

2 The red rod is half the length of the purple rod.

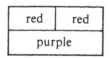

The white rod is "half of" the red rod; the light green rod is "half of" the dark green rod; the yellow rod is "half of" the orange rod. (The children appeared to grasp this concept easily.)

4

IV
A close look at the white cube
Directions from Lore and children's responses:

1 Lore: Select one of the little white blocks from your collection of rods. This is called a *cube*.

2 Lore: Press the face of the cube against the fleshy part of your thumb or your arm. The shape you see is called a square.

3 Lore: Make a stamp of the edge of the cube on your hand. What do you see?
Children: A line. ___

4 Lore: Press the corner of the cube against the fleshy part of your thumb or arm. What do you see?
Children: A dot. A point. ●

5 Lore: How many "faces" does the white cube have? [Children's answers ranged between four and seven.]

6 Lore then held up a white cube and asked the children to count the faces.

V
Comments
Jeff and Anne were able to measure with a ruler (centimeter scale) and read off the heights of the pyramids they built during free play. Jeff found not only that his pyramid was 21 centimeters high, but also that it was made up of 21 layers of rods.

About half of the children participated easily in some oral responses to these problems: $3 + 3 = \square$; $4 + 2 = \square$; $5 + 1 = \square$. These were introduced in the course of the discussion about the rods.

Recognizing geometric solids
Recognizing numerals

I
Review and extension of learning about the cube
Lore held up a large wooden cube.

> **1** Lore: What is the name we gave this shape?
> Children: Cube.

> **2** Lore: How many faces does it have? [The children counted as Lore marked each face with chalk.]

> **3** Lore: What is the shape of each face?
> Children: A square.

A pile of geometric solids (rectangular prisms, cubes, cones, triangular prisms, cylinders, etc.) was placed on a large table. The children sorted the solids into cubes and non-cubes. They observed that a cube has square faces only, while other prisms have combinations of square and non-square faces.

Lore drew pictures of a circle, a rectangle, a square, and a triangle on the chalkboard. The children named them all except the rectangle.

II
Numeral recognition and associated group size
The group played a numeral card game.

> **1** Lore held up a numeral card. Each child had to show "that many fingers." If the numeral card for seven was held up, the child would show seven fingers.

2 Each child was given a package of numeral cards (one numeral card for each number from 0 through 10). When Lore wrote a numeral on the chalkboard, the children held up the corresponding numeral card and named the number.

III
Free play with Cuisenaire® rods
The children built patterns, towers, trains, etc.

Counting
Recognizing number groups
One-to-one correspondence

I
Dice game

The purposes of this game were as follows:

1 To diagnose the children's systems of counting.

2 To give experience in recognizing a number group instantly.

3 To establish the concept of one-to-one correspondence by relating the number of dots on a die face to a collection of cubes.

4 To observe the children's ability to follow group instructions.

5 To give opportunities for mental subtraction.

The materials for each child were one die and a paper cup containing 20 white cubes from the Cuisenaire® rod collection.

The activity proceeded as follows:

1 The children were instructed first to place the die on the table (home position), then on signal to shake the die in both cupped hands, and drop the die on the table.

2 Each child was told to take from his own paper cup the number of cubes corresponding to the number of dots on the side of the die which was up.

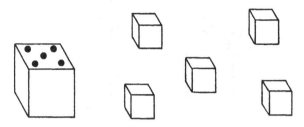

The group played another game, similar to the one described above. We call it Sub-game 1.

1 Lore wrote each child's name on the chalkboard. As a child's name appeared on the chalkboard, that child was to tell the number of cubes left in his cup.

All children were able to recognize their names as they were written on the chalkboard, and they could also give the number of cubes they had left. Most of the children counted by 1's.

2 Lore: Who could get rid of all his cubes on the next throw? Who could not finish on the next throw?

About three children immediately indicated that those who held the larger number of cubes could not finish on the next throw; those with only one or two cubes could finish on the next throw.

3 After a child's performance was approved, he placed the cubes he had taken from his cup in the large container in the middle of his table.

4 After the children had practiced shaking and dropping the dice for about a minute and a half, they played this game for approximately 15 minutes.

They found no difficulty in following instructions and performing the operations. Most of them took the cubes from the cups by counting 1, 2, 3, 4, etc. One boy (Louis) during several runs of the game counted by 2's, and during one run he counted by 3's. Noticeably, he grouped the cubes just as the dots were grouped on the die—two groups of 3 equal one group of 6.

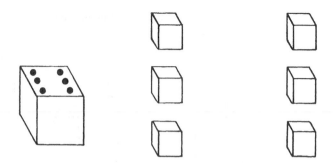

The group played Sub-game 2.

1 After one run of the basic game (dropping die, removing cubes from cup, etc.) Lore asked each child to tell what he had left after taking away the correct number of cubes.

Audrey had 7 cubes before this run; she removed 3 cubes; how many left? [4 cubes]

Some children, when asked the number of cubes they had left in their cups, answered immediately. Others had to count the cubes in their cups. Those with a smaller number of cubes (one to seven) had no difficulty. A few children had difficulty with the larger numbers.

David C. originally had 9 cubes left, but when he presumably removed 4 cubes during the last run, he answered, "One block left."

Dan B. originally had 11 cubes; he removed 4 cubes but could not tell how many he had left.

2 Lore continued this game for five to eight minutes, attempting to have each child dispose of all of his cubes. It seemed likely that a few of the children removed all their cubes from their cups sooner than they should have.

II
Free play with rods and geoboards (15 minutes)

From the children who volunteered to build with the rods, two (Rodney and Gary) were picked to build a tower, and then to measure its height with a meter stick. They were able to read "52 centimeters" as the height of their tower at the end of free play. From the other children who volunteered to build with rods, two (Audrey and Fred) were picked to build a tower and measure its height with the meter stick.

1 Audrey, unable to read "40 centimeters," responded by saying, "Four." The height of her tower was 41 centimeters. She understood Lore's explanation, "Forty plus one equals forty-one." Audrey's tower was built of an irregular system of rods. In "height" play—building "towers" with rods—some children build structures that are carefully planned, using long rods as the base and small rods at the top of a tower. Other children, like Audrey in this case, do not work in such a systematic fashion, e.g., a "tower" might have a mixture of long and small rods from the base to the top.

2 Fred, unable to read 37 centimeters, responded by saying, "Forty." Lore explained the correct reading—"37 centimeters." Fred used a systematic color scheme in building his tower.

Recognizing number groups
Diagnostic chalkboard session

I
Game of Lotto

Lore gave each child a Lotto card composed of nine different groups of items, each group containing a different number of items. On each table, there were several paper cups containing small paper squares, enough to provide nine squares for each child.

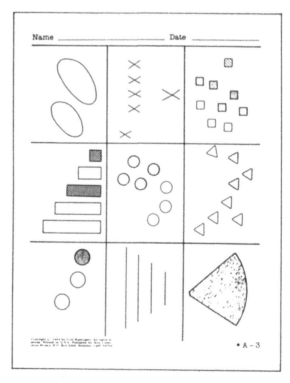

The game proceeded as follows:

1 Lore: When I hold up a numeral card, place a paper square over the group of items that corresponds to the numeral on the card.

2 Lore held up a card with the numeral 9 written on it. Each child looked at his Lotto card to find a section containing a group of nine items. If he found a "nine group," he placed a paper square on that section of his Lotto card.

The children followed instructions; few errors were made.

II
Free play with Cuisenaire® rods
Most of the children played with the rods.

III
Diagnostic chalkboard session

While the majority of the group were engaged in building with the rods, Lore selected for a diagnostic chalkboard session six children who appeared to have entered first grade with some skills in arithmetic.

Lore presented two sets of problems, problems in addition and subtraction:

1 The children volunteered to "make true" the following mathematical sentences written on the chalkboard by filling in the empty frames with the correct numeral:

(a) $3 + 2 = \square$ (d) $\square = 4 + 3$

(b) $2 + 2 = \square$ (e) $\square = 5 - 1$

(c) $\square = 4 + 1$ (f) $\square = 2 + 2 + 2$

2 Lore had to explain problem e: "Take one from five. (From a group of five white cubes take away one cube.) How many cubes are left?"

And problems of continuing the series:

3 Lore asked the children to tell her the missing numbers in the following series:

$$14, \quad 16, \quad 18, \quad \square$$

The children wrote 20 in the box to continue this series of consecutive even integers.

$$33, \quad 35, \quad 37, \quad \square, \quad \square$$

The children wrote 39 in the box following 37; then 41 in the second box to continue this series of consecutive odd integers.

The children were able to solve the problems presented during this session with little help from Lore.

Counting
One-to-one correspondence

I
Written exercises

Lore gave each child a lab sheet titled "How Many?" (lab sheet A4).

1 Children were to write in the small block the numeral that corresponded to the number of items in the large block.

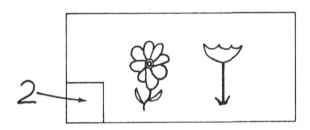

2 Children were to draw a picture in the large block to correspond with the numeral in the small block.

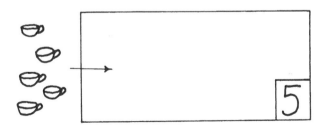

3 Some of the children did not understand the directions. Some had trouble writing numerals (such as 7, 5, 9, 6) but had

15

little or no trouble counting. Lore helped those who had difficulty with the sheet.

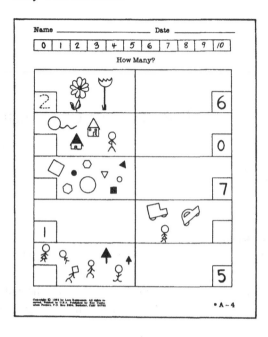

Those children who finished the first lab sheet were given a second one.

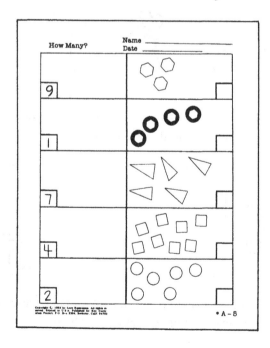

Eight of the children had no difficulty with the left column of lab sheet A5, but there was an average of three errors in the right column.

II

Free play with rods

The children built flat patterns, towers, etc. One child (David C.) constructed a very tall building with a large base and a small top. He worked with great care. Two children (Eric and David G.) working together devised a very intricate flat pattern.

Work with Cuisenaire® rods

I
Introduction: building "color stairs"

A pile of assorted rods was placed on each table. Lore asked the group to make "color stairs" with the rods.

> **1** Eight or nine children responded immediately. Their work served as models for other children who did not understand the directions Lore gave.

> **2** When all of the children had built their color stairs, Lore proceeded with a game.

II
First game

The children followed Lore's instructions.

> **1** Lore: Leave your color stairs in place.

> **2** Lore: From the pile of rods on your table, take one white rod, one light green, one red, one purple.

> **3** Lore: Place these rods in your hands; cup your hands and shake well. Put your hands behind your back. Feel each rod carefully.

> **4** Lore: Show me the biggest rod, the smallest rod, the rod that is half as big as the red one, the light green rod.

At Lore's signal, "Show me the biggest rod," each child held up the purple rod; then returned it to the collection of rods in the hand behind his back.

5 Lore: Now add the yellow rod to the collection of rods in your hand.

Lore asked Anne to come to the front of the room and "be the teacher." Continuing the procedure of the game, Anne asked the class to show her the following rods: the red rod, the yellow rod, the light green rod. The children followed Anne's instructions. Only a few children had difficulty.

III
Second game
The game was played as follows:

1 Using demonstration board to hold the rods, Lore made color stairs with the demonstration rods. As she built the stairs, she asked the group to answer, "What rod comes next?" Group response was good.

2 Lore, picking up a white demonstration rod, said, "Help me climb the stairs with the white rod."

Moving up the color stairs with the white rod—from one "step" to the next—Lore showed that the common difference between each adjacent rod is one white rod.

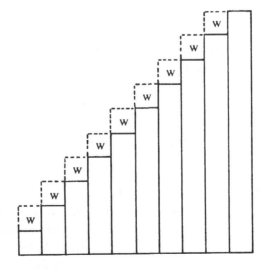

3 Lore picked up a yellow rod and asked Lynn how many white rods make one yellow rod. Lynn said that four white rods make one yellow rod.

Then Lore asked Lynn and the others in the group to prove how many white rods make one yellow rod.

Each child picked up a yellow rod from his collection of Cuisenaire® rods and "measured" it with the white rods. His rod model was proof that the yellow rod is as long as five white rods placed end to end.

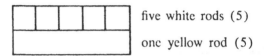

five white rods (5)

one yellow rod (5)

The children then measured the light green rod and proved that it is "three whites long."

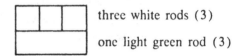

three white rods (3)

one light green rod (3)

The black rod is as long as seven white rods.

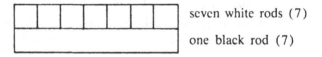

seven white rods (7)

one black rod (7)

4 Lore wrote several numerals on the chalkboard. Pointing to each numeral, she asked, "What color rod goes with _____ (numeral)?"

As Lore pointed to each numeral, the children held up the corresponding rod. For example, if she pointed to 8, the children held up the brown rod, which is as long as eight white rods placed end to end.

5 The numerals were left on the chalkboard. Lore asked several children, one at a time, to come to the chalkboard and: (a) select the rod from the set of demonstration rods that corresponds to a particular numeral; (b) stand that rod on the ledge of the chalkboard, beneath the numeral.

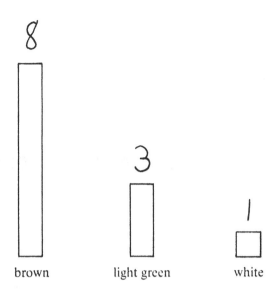

8	3	1
brown	light green	white

IV
Free play with rods

Children constructed flat patterns, towers, etc. Lynn and Audrey worked together. Lore noticed that Lynn had started to work out a pattern using a combination of different color rods to equal the length of the orange rod. Lore suggested that one blue rod and one white rod, end to end, would equal one orange rod. Lynn and Audrey developed the following patterns.

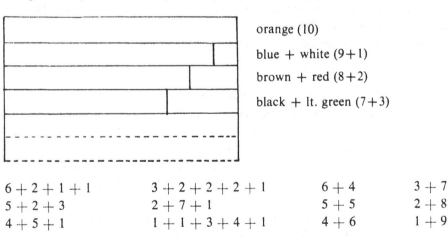

orange (10)

blue + white (9+1)

brown + red (8+2)

black + lt. green (7+3)

6 + 2 + 1 + 1	3 + 2 + 2 + 2 + 1	6 + 4	3 + 7
5 + 2 + 3	2 + 7 + 1	5 + 5	2 + 8
4 + 5 + 1	1 + 1 + 3 + 4 + 1	4 + 6	1 + 9

This list represents the rod patterns built by the children. Lore did not request the mathematical notation (8 + 2) for the rod train made out of a brown rod and a red rod placed end to end.

Counting
One-to-one correspondence

I
Pre-class game:
"How many children present?"

Whenever possible and profitable, use opportunities for counting children in interesting situations.

The children told Lore that eight children were absent today. Lore asked, "If there are eighteen in the whole class, and eight are absent, how many are present?"

The children's answers included seven, eight, nine, ten. Two children (Jeffrey and Anne) answered, "Ten."

Lore said that she could use her demonstration rods to determine how many children were present today.

1　As she placed her white rods in a row on the demonstration board, the children counted orally with her: one, two, three.

2　Then Lore asked them to count silently as she continued placing white rods in the row. When she had placed six white rods in the row, she asked, "How many?" The children answered, "Six."

3　Lore proceeded in this manner. When she had placed 10 white rods in the row, she asked, "How many?" The children answered, "Ten."

4　Lore then placed an orange rod on top of the row of white rods. (The orange rod is as long as 10 white rods placed end to end.)

5   Then she continued to add white rods to the row and the children resumed silent counting. When Lore had placed 18 white rods in the row she asked, "How many?" The group responded, "Eighteen."

6   Lore: There are 18 children in the whole class, and we have 18 white rods in the row. We can let one white rod stand for each child. I am going to remove from the row a white rod for each child who is absent today.

   As the children named each absentee, Lore removed a white rod from the row.

7   When eight white rods representing the absentees had been removed, Lore asked, "If there are eighteen children in the whole class, and if there are eight children absent today, how many children are present?"

   The children, with great enthusiasm, exclaimed, "Ten!"

8   Lore: Let's see if that is really true.

   She then had each child, one at a time, take one of the remaining white rods from the row on the demonstration board. When every child had taken "his rod," Lore asked, "Is it true that if eight children are absent from a class of eighteen, then ten children are present?"

   The children answered, "Yes!"

9   Lore wrote the following problem on the chalkboard:

$$\begin{array}{r} 18 \\ -8 \\ \hline 10 \end{array} \qquad 18 - 8 = 10$$

   Lore: If we start with a group of 18, and take away a group of 8, then we have a group of 10 remaining.

   Lore explained that the digit "1" in the numeral "18" means one group of ten, and that the digit "8" in the numeral "18" means one group of eight. The numeral "18" means a group of ten (1 ten) plus a group of eight (8 ones). She demonstrated this with the collection of rods used to solve the original problem presented to the group today.

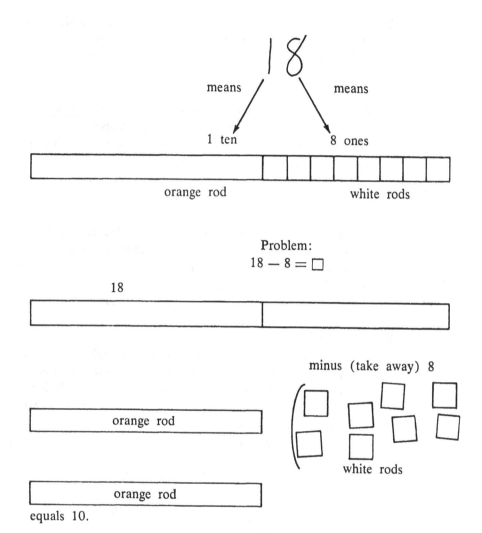

means   means

1 ten   8 ones

orange rod   white rods

Problem:
$$18 - 8 = \square$$

18

minus (take away) 8

orange rod

white rods

orange rod

equals 10.

Problem Solved:
$$18 - 8 = 10$$

II
Numeral card game

Lore had a bundle of numeral cards (11 cards per bundle, numerals from 0 to 10) for each child. The numerals in each bundle were out of the regular counting order. Each child was given a set of cards and instructed to sort them.

1   Lore: Start with the numeral for the lowest (smallest) number; arrange the numerals from the smallest to the largest (the numeral for the smallest number represented to the numeral for the largest number represented).

2   The children had almost no difficulty with this. Some children were confused by the left-to-right order:

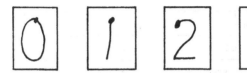

left-to-right

Peter was slow to start, but after beginning he had no difficulty. Bobby confused the left-to-right order but arranged numerals from 0 to 10 in a right-to-left order. Lore showed him the proper order for the numeral card arrangement.

Lynn confused the left-to-right order. At one point she had the 1 card between 6 and 8. She corrected her error.

Eric could not put cards in the proper order without help. He placed his cards in reverse order: 0, 1, 9, 8, 7, 6, 5, 4, 3, 2, 10. Lore explained what should be done.

III
Game of Lotto

Lore gave each child a Lotto card with nine groups of objects, each group containing a different number of objects (lab sheet A2).

1   Lore: In each block, place the numeral card that corresponds to the number of items in that block. The numeral card for 8 should be placed in the block containing eight items. The card for 6 should be placed in the block containing six items.

2   The children were able to do this with little difficulty. Cliff

finished quickly. Bobby still had trouble recognizing the difference between the numerals 9 and 6. Other children finished quickly.

Four children at one table started a new game—placing rods on the Lotto card, a brown rod on a block containing eight items, a red rod for a group of two, etc.

IV
Free play with rods

Special observation: Lynn remembered the patterns she had built the previous day. Without help she arranged the rods systematically in an ascending order, beginning with the orange rod and continuing to the white rod (the color stairs). Then she built the pattern illustrated below.

w	blue	
red	brown	
lt. green	black	
purple	dark green	
yellow	yellow	
dark green	purple	
black	lt. green	
brown	red	
blue	w	
orange		

Recognizing geometric solids
Counting

I
Game

Lore gave each child a geometric solid to hold behind his back. The child was to feel the form and then identify it.

1 Solids used were triangular prism, cube, cylinder (a large one and a small one), pyramid (large, small), sphere, and cone.

2 Some of the children could not give the exact name for a form but said that the form they held

"is like a church steeple,"

"is like a telephone pole,"

or "is like a ball."

When a child did not know the name for a particular solid, Lore told him the correct name: "A cylinder is a cylinder, whether it is large or small."

II
Free play

Some children played with the Dienes multibase blocks (base four). Others played with a large hollow wooden cube containing ten trays, one hundred smaller cubes in each tray. Lore worked with several of the children individually.

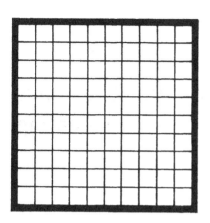

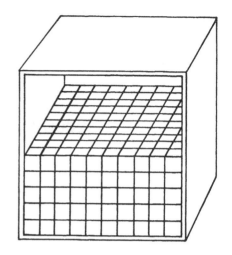

Tray of 100 small white cubes; ten such trays fit into the hollow cube

Large hollow wooden cube half filled with trays

1 When Lore asked the children to find the number of cubes on each tray, one boy (David C.) began counting by ones. When he reached 89, 90, 91, he lost count. Then he counted the number of rows of cubes (ten rows, ten cubes in each row) in the tray and he knew immediately that the tray held 100 cubes "because," he said, "ten 10's make 100."

2 Lore put another tray containing 100 cubes on top of the first tray: "How many?" she asked. David hesitated, then said, "Two hundred."

three trays of 100	300
three trays of 100 and one row of 10	310
four trays of 100, two rows of 10 and nine individual cubes	429

Lore showed David the numeral notation for the model they had built:

$100 + 100 = 200$
$100 + 100 + 100 = 300$

$$100 + 100 + 100 + 10 = 310$$
$$100 + 100 + 100 + 100 + 10 + 10 + 9 = 429$$

David appeared to comprehend this.

3 Eric counted the cubes in the tray of 100. He had difficulty because he would skip one cube or more in a series as he counted. Lore suggested that he use chalk to mark each cube as he counted it. Eric, proceeding to count, had no difficulty up to 40; then he could not remember the groups of 10; he had to start at 10 and count "10, 20, 30, 40 . . ."; then he realized that the next group of 10 would make 50. He proceeded this way, always having to count from 10 to know that 60 comes after 59; 70 comes after 69, etc. He continued counting until he had counted 99 white cubes. He did not know that 100 follows 99. Lore explained that 99 means "nine groups of 10 plus a group of nine 1's, and that if another cube is added to the group of nine 1's, the total is ten groups of 10, or 100."

4 Fred had no trouble counting the cubes in the tray of 100 from one to one hundred. But when Lore placed one cube representing "1" on top of the tray of 100, Fred called it "200"; two cubes and one tray he called "300" . . . one tray and ten cubes he called "1,000." Lore explained that one tray, ten cubes is "110" ($100 + 10 = 110$); one tray, one cube is "101" ($100 + 1 = 101$); one tray, two cubes is "102" ($100 + 2 = 102$), etc. Fred appeared amazed at this "new discovery." He asked, "Well, how do you get to 1,000?" Lore began putting trays on top of each other. Fred counted with her: 100, 200 . . . 500 . . . 1,000. *Ten* trays of 100 cubes equal 1,000 cubes ($10 \times 100 = 1000$).

5 Louis, Anne, and Audrey were able to understand this counting system; they could understand that one tray of 100 plus 10 cubes equal 110.

Other children built towers, patterns with Dienes multibase blocks.

Counting: tally method
Work with Cuisenaire® rods

I
Arithmetic work for Gary

Lore: How would you like to send Gary, who is ill, some arithmetic? The children said that they would like that.

1 Each child was given a piece of construction paper. Lore told them how to fold the paper to make a "book."

2 Lore: One thing that we can do is *tallying*. [Although no other tallying references occur in the classroom notes, it is recommended that the teacher repeat such experiences.]

On the Chalkboard	Lore's questions and children's answers
|||	Lore: What do you think this is? Children: Three.
||||	Lore: What do you think this is? Children: Four.
卌	Lore explained how we indicate five.

~~IIII~~ I = 6 ~~IIII~~ II = 7 ~~IIII~~ III = 8 ~~IIII~~ I III = 9	Children would say the name for the number as Lore placed the tallies on the chalkboard. Children had no difficulty.
~~IIII~~ ~~IIII~~	Peter knew that this means ten.
I = 1 ~~IIII~~ I = 6 II = 2 ~~IIII~~ II = 7 III = 3 ~~IIII~~ III = 8 IIII = 4 ~~IIII~~ IIII = 9 ~~IIII~~ = 5 ~~IIII~~ ~~IIII~~ = 10	Children did tallying on folded paper and made "tally books" to send to Gary.

II
Rod game:
Patterns of the yellow rod
A pile of assorted rods was placed on each table.

1   Lore: Take away all rods that are bigger or longer than the yellow rod.

2   Lore: Using the rods which are left, make as many patterns as you can.

3   Some examples of patterns developed by individual children are listed below. In these examples the white rod is the unit. If the white rod stands for 1, then the red rod stands for 2; the light green stands for 3; the purple 4; the yellow 5.

Jeff: 5 (yellow)
4 + 1 (purple plus white)
1 + 4 (white plus purple)
3 + 2 (light green plus red)
2 + 3 (red plus light green)

David C.: 5 (yellow)
4 + 1 (purple plus white)
3 + 2 (light green plus red)

2 + 3 (red plus light green)
1 + 3 + 1 (white plus light green plus white)

Ben: 5 (yellow)
2 + 2 + 1 (red plus red plus white)
2 + 1 + 2 (red plus white plus red)
4 + 1 (purple plus white)
1 + 1 + 3 (white plus white plus light green)

Lynn developed 11 patterns.
Louis developed 9 patterns.
David G. developed 14 patterns.

Cuisenaire® rods
Counting
One-to-one correspondence

I
Rod games

Materials used were a paper plate containing nine different color rods for each child (one rod missing from a set of 10) and a Lotto card for each child. Cards contain nine different groups of symbols, each group containing a different number of symbols.

Procedure for first part, "What color is missing?"

1 Lore: See what's wrong with the collection of rods you have.
One child (Bobby) replied immediately, "One is missing."
Another child (David G.) replied immediately, "My yellow one is missing."

2 Lore, going to each child, asked, "What color is your missing rod?" and "How many white cubes long is your missing rod?"
Each child responded individually. A few could not answer. (Eric, slow to discover the color of his missing rod, could not say "how many whites . . .").
When a child answered, Lore would give him his missing rod.

Procedure for the second part was as follows:

1 Lore gave each child a Lotto card.

2 Instructions to children—in each section place the rod that corresponds with the number of items in that section (e.g., yellow rod in section picturing five items; dark green rod in section with six items, etc.; the white rod was the unit).

Two children (Audrey and Eric) carefully took white (1) rods to measure the length of each rod, then placed the rods in their proper places.

Ben used a systematic approach. Starting with the white rod, he found the corresponding place on his Lotto card, then the red for 2, the light green for 3, etc.

Fred, in a random fashion, picked up a rod, looked at the groups of items, placed the rod very rapidly and erred about four times.

Most of the children worked with speed and confidence. Few had difficulty.

Procedure for the third part was as follows:

1 Lore: Louis, come to the front of the room and be the assistant teacher.

Lore asked Louis to take the yellow rod and the purple rod (large demonstration rods) and to place them end to end on the demonstration board. Louis put them one on top of the other. Lore explained to Louis and the group what is meant by *end to end.*

yellow	purple

2 Lore: Now everybody take a black rod, a green rod, and a white rod. Place them end to end.

Most of the group was slow to start; Ben, Audrey, and a few others immediately placed the rods end to end in the order in which they were called.

3 Lore continued with instructions for the children to build the following rod "trains." (She explained that they should start the series on the left and proceed from left to right.)

orange, purple, yellow
black, red, orange, blue
white, yellow, dark green, purple, light green
orange, brown, black, dark green, yellow, purple, light green

Gradually, as Lore increased the number of rods in a series, the children caught the idea and could remember the sequence of colors called; more than half the group could remember sequences involving as many as seven rods.

II
Free play with rods
Lore worked with Anne on an individual problem.

1 Lore: Make a train with the rods starting with the smallest and continuing to the longest. What do we have?

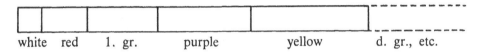

white   red   1. gr.   purple   yellow   d. gr., etc.

2 Lore: Take the white rod and place it on the table. Now take the red rod; place a white rod and a red rod end to end. Find a rod that is as long as the white rod and the red rod end to end. [The light green rod is the correct one.]

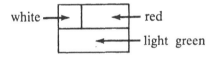

3 Now place a white rod, a red rod, and a light green rod end to end. Find a rod that is as long as the white rod, the red rod, and the light green rod end to end. [This is the dark green rod.]

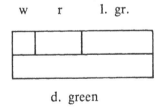

d. green

4 Lore showed Anne how to give numeral names to the rods. Let the white rod be called 1, then the red rod is 2.

5 Lore then tested Anne. She told Anne to build a certain "train," then to find one rod that is as long as that train, and, giving number names to the rods, to read off the problem illustrated.

Train	as long as	Problem
red and light green rods	yellow	$2 + 3 = \Box$
zero and white rods	white	$0 + 1 = \Box$
white and red rods	light green	$1 + 2 = \Box$
light green and purple rods	black	$3 + 4 = \Box$

Work with Cuisenaire® rods

I
Written work for small group

Eight children (Louis, Audrey, Anne, Ruthie, Fred, Danny, Peter, and David) were grouped together and given a sheet with addition problems.

1 Examples of problems:

$$\square = 7 + 3 \qquad 3 + \square = 8 \qquad 2 + 2 + 3 + 3 = \square$$

2 Cuisenaire® rods were available for children to build models of the problems.

Louis did the work without the use of rods; he worked rapidly, with confidence.

Audrey worked rather slowly; she appeared "unsure" at times (used rods).

Anne used rods in solving problems, but she worked rapidly.

Ruthie worked at moderate speed, using rods for some problems.

Fred worked slowly; he appeared sure of his work.

Peter worked slowly, deliberately, using rods.

David C. used rods, placing them over problems; he left all rod models on the page as proof of his correct answers.

Danny B. worked without rods most of the time; he had no difficulty.

II
Addition game

A pile of assorted Cuisenaire® rods was placed on each table and children were given paper plates.

1 Lore: For this game, the white rod stands for 1.

She then held up a problem card but covered the second numeral with her hand.

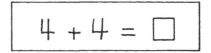

2 Lore: [pointing to the first numeral '4' on the problem card] Find the rod that stands for four and put it in your plate.

Children placed a purple rod in their plates.

3 Lore: [uncovered the second numeral, '4', on the problem card] Find the rod that stands for this number.

Children picked a purple rod and placed it in their plates.

4 Lore: Put them [a purple rod and a purple rod] end to end. What rod is as long as these?

Immediately Ben held up a brown rod. He proved that the two purple rods end to end are as long as the brown rod:

purple	purple
brown	

5 Lore wrote on the chalkboard $4 + 4 = 8$; then she asked one child (Lynn) to read what she had written.

Lynn was able to read the problem, except that she misread the plus (+) sign as "equals." Pointing out Lynn's error, Lore showed the children how to write the plus sign (+) and how to write the equal sign (=). Using her demonstration rods, she pantomimed "plus" (putting rods end to end) and "equal" (measuring a "train" of rods with another rod):

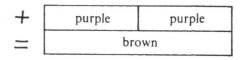

6 Lore held up another problem card:

$$2 + 3 = \square$$

Lore: Empty your plate. Get the rod for 2. Get the rod for 3. Place them end to end. How long?

Each child made a model—a red rod (2) end to end with a light green rod (3); measured the "train" and found the answer rod to be the yellow (5).

Ben looked at his rod model, then at the problem card and read, "two plus three equals five."

7 Lore used three more problem cards and the children built the rod models suggested by the problems on each card.

$$9 + 1 = \square$$

$$5 + 4 = \square$$

$$4 + 6 = \square$$

III
Free play

Children were free to select and build with a large assortment of materials available in the classroom.

Work with Cuisenaire® rods
Addition

I
Rod game

Materials for each child were:

> 10 white rods
> 3 light green rods
> 5 red rods
> 2 purple rods
> 1 each of dark green, black, brown, blue, orange

Procedure was as follows:

1 Lore: How many of each color rod do you have?

Children began counting; Rodney used systematic approach by grouping each color rod (all of the white rods together; all of the red rods together, etc.) and counting the number of rods in each group. Lore called the group's attention to this.

2 After most of the children had finished counting the rods in their individual collections, Lore recorded on the chalkboard the number of rods of each color each child should have:

On chalkboard	Color	Number of rods
with white chalk	white	10
with red chalk	red	5
with light green chalk	green	3
etc.		

Each child checked his own rod collection. When he was

sure that his collection was complete, he placed the rods in a paper plate.

Lore used letter symbols to represent each color rod. She asked, "What rod do you think this letter (*r* on chalkboard) stands for?" Children answered, "Red." Lore continued writing letter symbols on the chalkboard and children matched the symbols with the rods:

G — dark green   r — red
br — brown   y — yellow
blu — blue   g — light green
p — purple   or — orange
b — black   w — white

1   Lore: Find a purple rod and a red rod; place them end to end. [One child, Lynn, did so immediately; others followed.]

2   Lore: Find a rod that is as long as these two rods.
     Children found that the dark green rod was as long as the purple and the red rod placed end to end.
     Lore: So the purple rod (4) plus the red rod (2) equals the dark green rod (6).

$$p + r = G$$
$$4 + 2 = 6$$

3   Lore continued this game with the children. She gave instructions like this:

Rods end to end	Rods as long as these	Then
G, w	b	$6 + 1 = 7$
y, r	b	$5 + 2 = 7$
2g, r	br	$3 + 3 + 2 = 8$

(When Lore gave instructions, she said, "Find the yellow rod plus the red rod . . . ." Children responded by placing a yellow rod and a red rod end to end. They knew that *plus* meant that rods should be placed end to end.)

4   Lore: Find a white rod. Find another white rod. Place them end to end. This is how we write *plus*.

$$1 + 1 = 2$$

Show me this with rods. [Three children (Lynn, Jeff, Louis) did this immediately; others followed.]

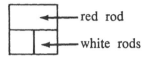

II
Game of addition

The materials for the game were several problem cards (3″ × 12″) with an addition problem on each card, together with numeral cards.

1 Lore: Get rods for this:

$$2 + 7 = \square$$

Children picked up a red rod and a black rod, put them end to end, and found the blue rod to be as long as the red and the black.

Lore placed a small numeral card on the problem card and held it up for the class to see:

$$2 + 7 = 9$$

2 Then she stood numeral cards 0 through 10 on the chalkboard ledge and held up different problem cards; children used rods to solve the problems and then gave the answer by picking the numeral card from the chalkboard ledge.

A few examples of the problems:

$$5 + 4 = \square \qquad 4 + 6 = \square$$
$$2 + 2 + 1 = \square \qquad 3 + 4 = \square$$
$$2 + 3 = \square \qquad 3 + 5 = \square$$

III
Special work

A small group (Audrey, Anne, Ruth, Louis) volunteered to work on problems from the chalkboard:

$3 + 7 = \Box$ $5 + 5 = \Box$ $2 + 2 + 3 + 1 = \Box$
$4 + 2 + 2 + 2 = \Box$ $3 + 3 + 3 + 1 = \Box$
$6 + 4 = \Box$ $1 + 1 + 1 + 1 + 1 + 1 = \Box$

1 In the problem $4 + 2 + 2 + 2 = \Box$ Anne immediately responded "10." In explanation of what she did, she said that she added $4 + 2 = 6$, then $2 + 2 = 4$. If $4 + 2 = 6$ and $2 + 2 = 4$, then

$$\underbrace{4 + 2} \quad + \quad \underbrace{2 + 2} = 10$$

because   6   +   4 $= 10$

2 Children caught the idea of adding *groups* of numbers; they knew in the problem $3 + 3 + 3 + 1 = \Box$ to add $3 + 3$, then add $3 + 1$; then

$$\underbrace{3 + 3} \quad + \quad \underbrace{3 + 1} = 10$$

6   +   4 $= 10$

Children could prove their answers by using rods.

orange			
dark green		purple	
light green	light green	light green	w

These examples seem to show an intuitive perception of the associative law of addition.

Counting
Work with rods

I
Pre-class game
The children counted those present.

1   Lore asked the children at each table, "How many present at this table?"

Six present at one table. Lore picked up a dark green rod to represent this group. Three present at another table (light green rod). One present on floor (white rod). One present "just came in" (white rod).

2   Demonstration rods—dark green, light green, white, white—were placed end to end on demonstration board:

dark green	light green	w	w
6	+ 3	+ 1	+ 1

Children "proved" this by placing orange rod (10) and white rod (1) end to end below this group of rods.

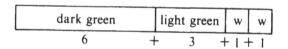

dark green	light green	w	w
orange			w

$$10 + 1 = 11$$

44

II
Rod game: "What's in the middle?"

Each child was given one wooden tube that measured the length of the orange (10) rod. Any rod could fit in the tube.

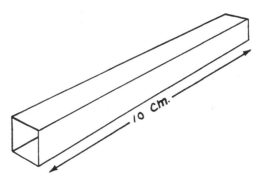

1 A box of rods was placed on each table. Children were allowed to discover that one orange rod or ten white rods exactly filled the tube.

2 Lore: Fill your tube with rods. [Children did this.] When the tube is full, hide with your fingers the color that can be seen at either end of the tube.

3 Lore (to Rodney): What color can be seen at one end of the tube.
   Rodney: Purple.

4 Lore (to group): Everybody take a purple rod. Now, what color is on the other end of the tube?
   Rodney: White.

5 Lore: Everybody take a white rod and place it end to end with the purple rod. What color rod is in the middle of Rodney's tube?
   Children: Yellow.

6 Lore checked Rodney's tube by holding it upright, one finger covering the bottom hole, then dropping the rods, one by one, into the tube. She found that the purple rod (4) plus the yellow rod (5) plus the white rod (1) equal the orange rod (10).

7 The game continued:

	one end	other end	in the middle
$3 + 6 + 1 = 10$	light green	white	dark green
$10 + 0 = 10$	orange	orange	0
$4 + 4 + 2 = 10$	purple	red	purple
$4 + 5 + 1 = 10$	purple	white	yellow
$2 + 8 = 10$	red	brown	0
$1 + 4 + 5 = 10$	white	yellow	purple
$4 + 3 + 1 + 2 = 10$	purple	red	light green, white

Of course, when more than three rods are placed in the tube, the variety of combinations is greatly increased, and more information is necessary to determine the colors in the tube.

III
Game

Materials for the game were a felt board with 100 squares and sponge "numeral cards" (numerals from 1 to 100).

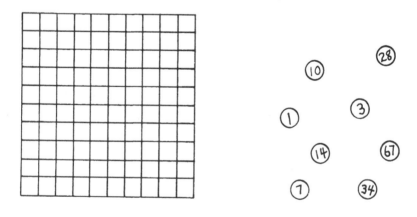

felt board   sponge numeral cards

1 Lore: Can you read?

Children could read these numerals:

Rodney	20
Ruth	81
Louis	79
Roland	94
David C.	97

2 Each child was given a sponge numeral card by Fred, who assisted Lore. Then the child was to place the numeral in its proper place on the felt board. Louis immediately observed that all of the *1*'s (11, 21, 31, etc.) would go under *1* in a column; that there was a column for *2*'s (12, 22, 32, 42, etc.), for *3*'s, *4*'s, etc. (This refers to numbers whose last digit is either *1*, *2*, etc.)

1		4						
11		14						
21		24						
31		34						
41		44						

October

Summary of Topics

Arithmetic operations
Number line
Numeral recognition
Inequalities
Counting
Geometric recognition
Sets
Graphing
Logic
Mixed operations
Discovering negative numbers
Word problems
Odd-even

Number line

I
Grasshopper game

Lore drew pictures of grasshoppers and a number line on the chalkboard.

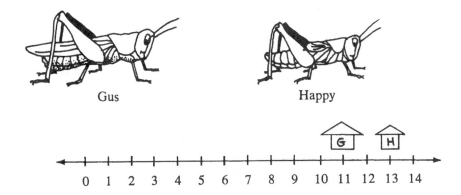

Gus   Happy

0 1 2 3 4 5 6 7 8 9 10 11 12 13 14

1 Lore: We shall build Gus's house at point 11 on the number line and Happy's house at point 13 on the number line. Gus and Happy had a race. Both Gus and Happy are at point 1 on the number line (or racetrack). Gus is to make jumps of 2 units. Happy is to make jumps of 1 unit.

2 Lore: Gus jumps from 1 to _____?
Children: Three.
Lore: Happy jumps from 1 to _____?
Children: Two.
Lore: Gus jumps from 3 to _____?
Children: Five.
Lore: Happy wants to catch up. How many jumps should she

make from 2?
Children: Three jumps.

3 Lore: Now Gus wants to get to 9. How far must he jump?
Children: Four units (2 jumps of 2 units); 5 + 4 = 9.
Lore: Happy wants to land 1 unit ahead of Gus. How far must she jump?
Children: Five units (5 jumps of 1 unit each); 5 + 5 = 10.

4 Lore: Gus is angry. "I'm going to Happy's house," he said, "and hide." From 9, how many units must he move to get to Happy's house (point 13)?
Jeffrey: Four.
Lore: Gus shut the door. Nobody can get inside. But Happy did not know what Gus did. So she decided to go to Gus's house. How many units is it to Gus's house? Happy is at 10.
Children: One unit; 10 + 1 = 11.

5 Lore: Now Gus and Happy are at each other's house waiting for the other to arrive. They wait and wait but nothing happens. They wait a little longer. Now they're tired of waiting. Gus says, "I'm going to move back 4 units." Where does he go?
Louis: To 9; 13 − 4 = 9.
Lore: Gus says, "I thought I'd find Happy, but she isn't here. Where is she?" Then he said, "Maybe she's farther back along the track." So Gus went all the way back to point 3. How many units did he move?
Anne: Five units
   Lore asked Anne to demonstrate on the blackboard the moves that Gus would have to take to get to 3. Anne did this and found that Gus would have to move 6 units or 3 jumps of 2 units each: 9 − 6 = 3; 3 + 6 = 9.

6 Lore: Now Gus decided maybe he'd better go home. How many moves to his house from 3?
Ruth, Audrey: Eight units or four jumps of 2 units each; 8 + 3 = 11.
Lore: When Gus got home, to his surprise, whom did he find waiting for him?
Children: Happy!

II
Children's independent activity

Children came to the chalkboard and made up their own number-line problems. They were able to do this with little assistance from Lore.

Number line	Equation

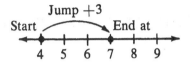

$$4 + 3 = 7$$

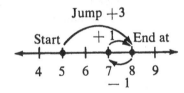

$$7 - 2 = 5$$

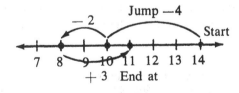

$$5 + 3 - 1 + 1 = 8$$

$$14 - 4 - 2 + 3 = 11$$

Number line
Geometric recognition
Numeral recognition

I
Grasshopper game

With the number line on the chalkboard, Lore continued the grasshopper game of the previous day. The children remembered the names given the grasshoppers.

1 Lore: Gus is at point 30 on the number line. He is going to point 32. This means he moves how many units?
Children: Two units.

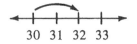

2 Lore: Happy is at point 40. She is going to move backward as many units as Gus moves forward. Where will she land?
Children: At 38.

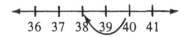

3 Lore: Gus takes another 2 steps (1 jump). Where is he now?
Children: At 34.

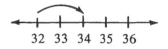

4 Lore: Happy takes another 2 steps (1 jump) backward. Where is she now?
Children: At 36.

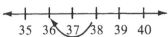

5 Lore: Gus wants to meet Happy. How many units must he move?
Children: Two.

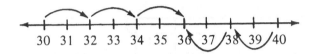

6 Lore: How many steps did Happy go?
Children: Four; 40 − 4 = 36.

7 Lore: How many steps did Gus go?
Children: Six; 30 + 6 = 36.

II
Game: What numerals are missing?

The felt board of 100 squares hanging on one wall of the classroom had some missing numeral sponges. Lore asked the group, "Which numerals are missing?"

1 Lore: What is the numeral for the lowest missing number?
Children: Ten
Lore: Which is the next lowest?
Children: Eleven
Lore: And the next lowest?
Children: Twenty-one
And so on.
Lore: What is the numeral for the largest number represented on the felt board?
Lynn: One hundred
Lore: Take 100 off the board.
Lore: Take off 70. Now take off 30. And 90, 50, 88, 77, 66, 95, 81, 92, 71, 65, 78, 79, 62, 80.

2 The children recognized numerals and located them on the felt board. A few children picked incorrect numerals and some children were slow, but the game moved swiftly. The children had no difficulty.

III
Game: Follow the leader (geoboards)

The children were given geoboards and rubber bands. Lore formed the following figures with rubber bands on the geoboard.

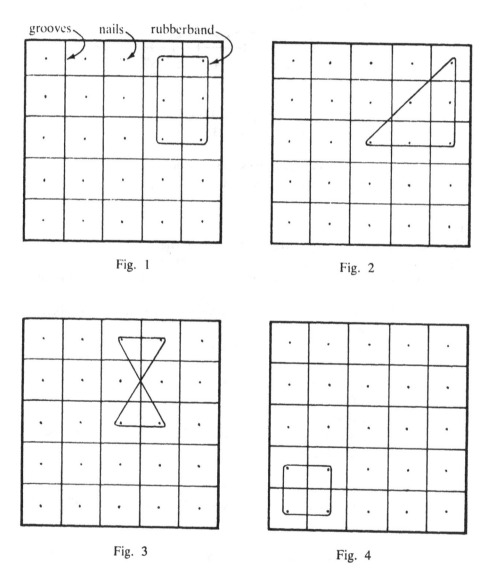

grooves   nails   rubberband

Fig. 1   Fig. 2

Fig. 3   Fig. 4

1   Most of the children were able to follow one part of the operation, making the correct form (shape) with a rubber band.

Children had difficulty with the dimensions of the form (for example, the triangle in Fig. 2 was made smaller than the one Lore made). Also, some children placed a particular form upside down, sidewise, etc.

2   Lore: What shapes are shown on the geoboard?

The children were able to recognize the shapes and give these answers: for Fig. 1, rectangle; for Fig. 2, triangle; for Fig. 3, "two triangles pointing to each other"; for Fig. 4, square.

IV
Varied activities

Some of the children continued to work on the geoboards. They formed various shapes and designs with rubber bands. Other children built with the rods.

A group of four children (Audrey, Anne, Ruth, and Louis) did written work (lab sheets C12 and C19). They used the rods in solving the problems.

Note: In retrospect, it seems that too many important teaching games were played on this day. They might have been distributed over a longer period.

Number line
Subtraction with Cuisenaire® rods

I
The number line goes on and on and on . . .
Lore continued the grasshopper game.

1   Lore: Just before you came into the room, the two grasshoppers, Gus and Happy, were jumping on the number line (on the chalkboard). They jumped and jumped all the way to point 64 on the number line. But there is no point 64 written on the number line on the chalkboard. Where do you think they jumped?

2   Puzzled expressions appeared on the children's faces as they looked about the room and began pointing outside the door.
     Then Lore led the group outside the classroom and into the hallway; she pointed to a spot on the wall.

3   Lore: The grasshoppers jumped all the way out here! Suppose they wanted to reach 100. About where do you think 100 would be?
     Children: Right outside the principal's office.

4   Lore: What about 500?
     Children: Up the hill!

5   Lore: And a million?
     Children: In the next town!
     The children realized that the fact that the number line in the classroom appeared to extend only to a certain point did not

mean that the number line stops. They understood that the line goes on and on and on in our imagination.

II
The minus sign
Lore demonstrated work with problem cards.

1 Problem cards with subtraction problems were available in the classroom. Lore held up a problem card.

$$6 - 2 = \Box$$

2 She then discussed the meaning of the minus sign (−) and explained that it means "take away." She demonstrated with rods:

If the white rod is one, then the rod for six is the dark green rod; the rod for two is the red rod.

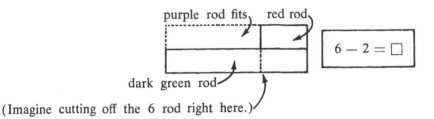

(Imagine cutting off the 6 rod right here.)

3 Lore passed out several problem cards and the children built rod models of the problems (as diagrammed above). When they found the "answer" rod, they placed that rod in the frame on the problem card.

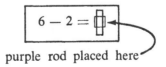

purple rod placed here

Inequalities
Counting

I
Guessing game 1
Which glass container has the greater number of marbles?

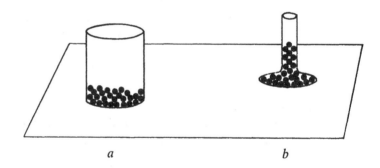

a   *b*

1   All the group except two (David C. and Gary) guessed that container *b* had more marbles than container *a*.

2   Lore placed one of the containers on each table and asked the children to count the marbles. They counted 36 marbles in container *a* and 36 marbles in container *b*.

3   The children explained that they thought container *b* had more marbles in it because of the shape (long, narrow) and because container *b* was full of marbles.

II
Guessing game 2

Which tray of cubes has the greatest number of cubes (pieces)? Which has the least number of pieces?

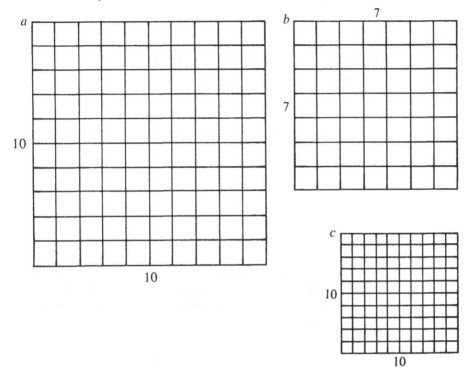

1 The children made all sorts of guesses about which tray had the greatest number of cubes until it was established that *a* and *c* had a greater number of pieces than *b*. [Both *a* and *c* contain 100 cubes even though *c* is smaller than *a*. Although *b* is larger than *c*, *b* contains only 49 cubes.]

2 The children were confused about the meaning of "least" number of cubes. Lore explained the meaning of "least." It was established that *b* had the least number of pieces.

3 Which tray has the largest amount of wood? Which has the least amount of wood?

    About half of the children realized that the largest tray of cubes *a* contained more wood than the other two trays. Some children voted for the two smaller trays. Lore explained why the largest tray had the most wood, the second largest tray had the second largest amount of wood, the smallest tray the least amount of wood, although the number of pieces of wood was the same in *a* and *c*.

III
Varied activities: children's choices
The children were allowed to build with several sets of blocks or work problems from the chalkboard.

1 Anne was able to do the following problems with no help.

$$6 + 3 = \square \qquad 4 + 2 + 1 = \square$$
$$43 - 3 = \square \qquad 9 + 9 + 1 = \square$$
$$9 - 3 = \square$$
$$8 + 4 = \square$$
$$25 - 10 = \square$$

2 Louis, working exceptionally fast, was able to do the problems below with no help. Lore simply gave him the idea on the multiplication problem; for example, 3×4 means three 4's added together.

$$6 + 3 = \square \qquad 9 + 9 + 1 = \square$$
$$43 - 3 = \square$$
$$4 \times 5 = \square$$
$$2 \times 10 = \square$$
$$3 \times 9 = \square$$
$$5 \times 3 = \square$$
$$25 - 10 = \square$$
$$5 \times 2 = \square$$
$$6 \times 1 = \square$$
$$3 \times 4 = \square$$

Cuisenaire® rods

I
Varied activities

Three children (Louis, Anne, and David C.) did individual written work. The rest of the class worked on problem cards.

1 Each child was given six problem cards. Cuisenaire® rods and numeral cards were available for use with the problem cards.

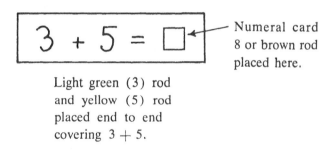

Numeral card
8 or brown rod
placed here.

Light green (3) rod
and yellow (5) rod
placed end to end
covering 3 + 5.

2 Here is a list of the problems included on lab sheets made up for October 10, 11, 12, 18.

$10 - 2 = \square$	$1 + 5 = \square$
$5 + 5 = \square$	$2 + 3 = \square$
$2 + 6 = \square$	$3 - 1 = \square$
$7 - 6 = \square$	$8 + 2 = \square$
$6 + 1 = \square$	$4 - 3 = \square$
$7 + 2 = \square$	$4 + 4 = \square$
$7 + 0 = \square$	$3 + 3 = \square$
$6 - 6 = \square$	$4 + 3 = \square$
$2 + 2 + 1 + 1 = \square$	$2 + 2 + 1 = \square$

63

$$8 - 2 = \square$$
$$5 + \square = 6$$
$$5 - 5 = \square$$
$$2 + \square = 8$$
$$10 - 0 = \square$$
$$5 + 3 = \square$$
$$5 + \square + 2 = 8$$
$$5 - \square = 3$$
$$10 - 7 = \square$$
$$7 + 3 = \square$$

Note: See lab sheets E1 thru E14

Addition and subtraction

I
Varied work for two groups of children

Seven children worked on individual lab sheets in their work folders. Each child was allowed to choose the lab sheet(s) in his work folder he wanted; each was also allowed to choose between doing problems with or without the use of rods.

The others in the class (except Jeff) worked on problem cards like the one diagrammed below:

$7-7$	$6+3$	$4+5$
$9+1$	$4+4$	$8-3$
$3-2$	$7-2$	$6+4$

1   Each child was given a problem card and a set of small numeral cards with numerals from 0 to 10. The correct numeral card was to be placed over a particular problem as the answer to that problem; for example, in the block with $4+5$, the child was to place the numeral card 9 over the problem.

The children had little difficulty with the addition problems; they had more difficulty with the subtraction problems.

2   One child (Jeff) did approximately 25 individual problem cards like this: $7+3=\square$.

Placing numeral cards in the answer frames, he laid out the problem cards, one by one, over a large area on the floor. Lore suggested this activity because she recognized Jeff's need for larger body movement.

II
Free play with Cuisenaire® rods

Addition and subtraction
Summary of work
Evaluation

I
Work with problem cards

Five children in the class worked on problem cards. They used Cuisenaire® rods and numeral cards as indicated below.

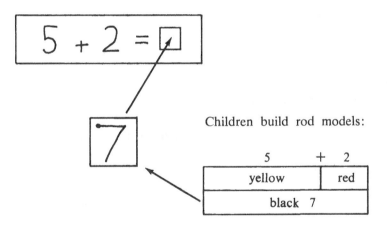

Children build rod models:

5	+	2
yellow		red
black 7		

Most of the children could do these problems. They did have difficulty with subtraction problems, possibly because the addition process as an outgrowth of play with rods was a more deliberate childlike activity than subtracting or "taking away." (During free-play sessions, the process of "putting rods end to end," or adding rods, was a natural and deliberate activity. More varied materials should have been used in the teaching of subtraction. Individual counters, groups of objects, etc., should have been used along with the rods.)

67

II
Summary of written work

Thirteen children took their individual notebooks to their seats when they entered the room. They were allowed to do any pages in their notebooks and to stop when they were tired. The practice of *asking* the first-graders to find and correct their mistakes of the previous day was *discontinued*. (See *Notes to Teachers*, Appendix C, page 35, for explanation of this change.) The notebooks are filled with new pages as needed. More difficult work is added or more practice is given on a particular level.

Child	1	2	3	4	5	6	7	8	9	10	11	12
Problems solved	9	17	18	21	26	27	31	32	37	41	46	71
Problems solved correctly	7	11	13	21	16	24	21	27	36	37	39	61

Eric's work is not included here.

III
Range of difficulty

All children were able to do problems such as

$5 + 3 = \square$; $6 + 4 = \square$;   and other addition problems.

Errors occurred in subtraction:

$9 - 5 = \square$; $8 - 6 = \square$; $6 - 6 = \square$;   and others.

Four children were able to do problems like these:

$1 + \square + 5 + 1 = 10$; $9 - \square = 2$

Three children figured out the use of frames in the problems below without the teacher's help:

$\square + \square = 8$; $\square + \square = 6$

One child was able to do the following problems:

$$6 \times 3 = \square; \quad \square \times 7 = 14$$
$$4 \times \square = 12$$
$$(2 \times 3) + (3 \times 3) = \square$$

With the aid of rods, six children can do addition and subtraction problems involving numbers from 0 through 20.

Comment: This is the first-grade class after one month of school. Rods are always on the table. Seven children already do much of the work without rods. (We are *not*, however, encouraging this at this time.)

The five children not included in this summary have not begun written work; four can do the problems slowly with rods when writing is not involved. Eric is one exception.

Thirteen children were able to write by October 12. On the first day of class there were six children writing. On the second day four more children were writing. On the third day three more children were writing.

IV
Evaluation

Many evaluations such as the following were made throughout the year but are not included. This sample evaluation will suffice for our purposes at this time.

Eric had been absent for several days. He is not making much progress. Today (as once before) he cried when given a job to do while I worked with other children. He was given a large card with this problem on it: $2 + 1 + 2 = \square$ and was asked to "build the rod train" that was suggested by the problem. After building the train, he was to find another rod with which to measure the train.

When I sat down with him, he could *read* the problem with ease but guessed at the rods. We put the card away and instead I had him build the "color stairs." He initially omitted several rods, but finally he put them all in sequence. When given another purple rod (1 purple rod = 4 white rods), however, he could not tell me how many whites "long" it was until he had measured it with white rods. This happened with *all* the other rods. He could identify them with a number name only after measuring them with whites. (He measured the purple rod *three* separate times.)

Eric is very anxious, but his face lights up when he is correct and he relates as long as I sit down with him. (Eric has a similar problem with his other work, and he seems to be without friends.)

Sets

I
Game

Lore called children to the front of the room in the following way:

1 All people who are *not* six years old come and stand by me.

2 All people who have a front tooth missing come and stand by me.

3 All people with red socks come and stand by me.

Then, on the chalkboard, these symbols and groupings were written:

Symbols   *Grouping*

not six   4 children
years old ⚤

                     3 🧍 (boys) + 1 🧍 (girl)

missing   🦷   8 children
tooth

                     2 🧍's + 6 🧍's

red socks 🧦   6 children

                     6 🧍's + 0 🧍's

white socks 　　　6 children

2 👦's + 4 👧's

Then Lore asked the following groups (sets) to stand:

Girls 　　　　　　　　　　　4 👦

Boys 　　　　　　　　　　　14 👧

(The children counted groups
of boys in various sections of
the room:
$3 + 2 + 2 + 1 + 3 + 3$)

Girls with white
socks, missing a tooth 　　　Ø 👦

Boys with red socks,
missing a tooth 　　　　　　Ø 👧

Boys *not* 6 years old
with white socks 　　　　　1 👧

Boys, *not* 6 years old
with socks *not* red,
socks *not* white,
missing tooth 　　　　　　　4 👧

Girls, *no* missing tooth,
socks *not* white, over
6 years old

∅ 🧍

Those who are both   (nobody   ∅
girls and boys   came up)

Boys with red and
white socks

5 🧍

Boys or girls not 6,   (nobody   ∅
and older than 6   came up)

Girls with 11 fingers

∅ 🧍

Boys with 9 fingers

∅ 🧍

Boys with blond hair

2 🧍

Boys with blond hair,
missing a tooth

1 🧍

Girls with green dresses

Boys with 5 buttons on shirt

II
Second game
Lore introduced another game:

    1   Lore: Behind my suitcase I hid half as much as two pencils.

    2   Children made various guesses: 3, 4, 2 pencils, etc. Lore explained "half of" by breaking a piece of chalk into two parts, one part "half of."

    3   Lore: I hid $(3 + 3 + 2)$ little red blocks. "How many little red blocks did I hide?"
        Lore went around the room and answers were whispered to her.

    4   Lore: I hid some pieces of paper, as much as half of ten.
        Children knew "5."
        On the chalkboard Lore showed one way to write "half of."

$$\tfrac{1}{2} \times 10 \quad \text{(half of ten)}$$
$$\tfrac{1}{2} \times 4 \quad \text{(half of four)}$$
$$\tfrac{1}{2} \times 100 \quad \text{(half of one hundred)}$$

III
Third game
Using the previous chalkboard games, Lore allowed the children to draw pictures and loops. The loops suggest subsets of many of the sets of elements included in the first game.

1 Lore: I am thinking of a girl, with a missing tooth, and white socks.

The children were to draw a picture of a girl, a missing tooth, and a white sock, and then to put a loop around the picture. The children, at their seats, drew more pictures suggested by Lore.

Elements	*Picture*
a balloon	
a boy	
a girl	
a big ear	
a boy in front of a house; boy holding a balloon	

a girl and a boy
holding hands

a boy and a girl,
both with big ears,
both holding balloons,
both standing beside
   a house

2   In retrospect it becomes apparent that this type of activity—
play with sets of things—should have been repeated throughout
the year.

Word problems: multiplication

I
Oral quiz

Lore asked the following questions. Children gave answers and explanations regarding their answers.

1 How many curly tails have seven pigs?

Seven. Each pig has one curly tail; seven pigs have seven curly tails: $(7 \times 1 = 7)$.

2 How many big ears have four dogs?

Eight. Each dog has two ears; four dogs have eight ears: $(4 \times 2 = 8)$.

3 How many legs have two chairs?

Eight. Each chair has four legs; two chairs have eight legs: $(2 \times 4 = 8)$.

4 How many hands have ten people?

Twenty. Each person has two hands; ten people have twenty hands: $(10 \times 2 = 20)$.

At this point Lore called ten children to the front of the room. "How many hands do they have altogether?" Children counted each child's hands, counting by 2's to 20 hands.

5 How many fingers have three people?

Thirty. Each person has five fingers on each hand or ten fingers; three people have thirty fingers: $[(5 + 5) \times 3 = 30]$, $[(2 \times 5) \times 3 = 30]$, $[(3 \times 10) = 30]$.

6 How many noses have 365 dogs?

365. Every dog has one nose; 365 dogs have 365 noses! $(365 \times 1 = 365)$.

II
Written work in individual folders
Lab sheets E1 through E14 were used.

III
Free play

Addition and subtraction

I
Oral and chalkboard work
The children practiced on names for six.

1 Lore demonstrated with rods to show how various combinations of rods can equal the length of the dark green (6) rod.

2 Several children came to the chalkboard and made up problems:

light green + red + white
$3 + 2 + 1 = 6$

light green + light green
$3 + 3 = 6$

orange — purple
$10 - 4 = 6$

blue — light green
$9 - 3 = 6$

II
Written work
Each child was given his notebook, which included a sheet to be used for making up problems that equal 6. The sheet is not included in the Mathematics Laboratory Materials. The teacher can make sheets like this for individual children.

$= 6$	$= 6$
$= 6$	$= 6$
$= 6$	$= 6$

Children's written responses to the lab sheet on combinations of 6 were very good. There were a number of complex equations involving addition and subtraction within the same equation, for example,

$(10 - 8 + 2 + 2 = 6)$; $(10 - 10 + 6 = 6)$; $(10 - 7 + 2 + 1 = 6)$

Other lab sheets in children's notebooks included subtraction problems.

III
Free play with Cuisenaire® rods

Multiplication using Cuisenaire® rods
Special work

I
Game: Hiding

The children were given paper plates containing the following rods: two each of the orange, blue, brown, black, dark green; three each of the yellow, purple; five each of the light green, red, white.

1 Lore: [with two paper cups; under each was a collection of rods] Under one cup I have three rods of the same color; under the other cup I have five rods of the same color. Both collections of rods when placed end to end (when I make a train out of the rods) are the *same length*. What are the rods?

Cup A   Cup B

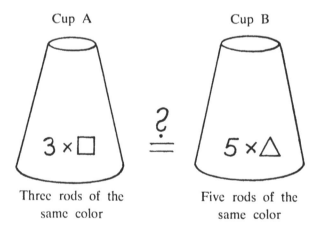

Three rods of the   Five rods of the
same color   same color

The children were very puzzled at first; they tried a variety of combinations. Anne found a correct combination first.

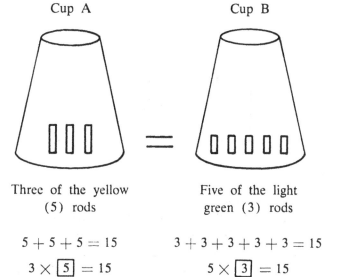

Cup A

Cup B

Three of the yellow (5) rods

Five of the light green (3) rods

$$5 + 5 + 5 = 15$$

$$3 \times \boxed{5} = 15$$

$$3 + 3 + 3 + 3 + 3 = 15$$

$$5 \times \boxed{3} = 15$$

Another possible solution:
Cup A: three orange (10) rods $3 \times 10 = 30$
Cup B: five dark green (6) rods $5 \times 6 = 30$

2 Lore proceeded with this game of hiding rods under two paper cups. Other problems are listed below.

Cup A		Cup B
$3 \times \square$	$=$	$4 \times \triangle$
$4 \times \square$	$=$	$2 \times \triangle$

3 The chart below shows the rod combinations found for the two problems listed above.

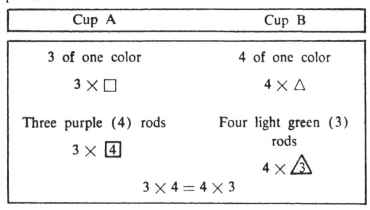

Cup A	Cup B
3 of one color	4 of one color
$3 \times \square$	$4 \times \triangle$
Three purple (4) rods	Four light green (3) rods
$3 \times \boxed{4}$	$4 \times \boxed{\triangle 3}$
$3 \times 4 = 4 \times 3$	

```
┌─────────────────────────────────────────────────────────┐
│   4 of one color              2 of one color            │
│                                                          │
│       4 × □                        2 × △                │
│                                                          │
│   Four red (2) rods          Two purple (4) rods         │
│                                                          │
│       4 × [2]                      2 × [4]               │
│              4 × 2 = 2 × 4                              │
└─────────────────────────────────────────────────────────┘
```

II
Written work

Several lab sheets with problems in addition, subtraction, and multiplication were spread out on a table. Children came to the table in groups of 3 to select individual lab sheets. When the children select their own work tasks, it cannot be predicted whether they will select a "follow-up" sheet—based on work just presented—or whether they will select unrelated material.

III
Special work

This special report is included as a sample of individual help for a child who does not function well within his group.

Eric was taken out of the classroom to another room where the two of us were alone. We sat down at a table together and placed a large selection of different color rods on the table. We worked first on Eric's recognition of the individual rods, for example, his association of a particular rod with its spoken and written number name. (For our purposes, the white rod was our unit.)

Eric was shown each color rod in turn. I asked, "How many white rods (1 rods) is this rod (yellow) long?" Eric used white rods to measure the yellow rod. He found that the yellow rod is as long as 5 white rods placed end to end. Then I asked Eric to pick up every other yellow rod he saw on the table. He did this, lining up all of the yellow rods (one at a time) alongside the 5 white rods. I pointed out that *all the yellow rods are as long as the yellow rod that is as long as 5 white rods.*

We followed this procedure with every other color rod until Eric was able to call out the correct number name for every rod I held up. He could do this with great speed. His only confusion at first was with these four rods: brown with orange; and black with blue. I told him to look at each rod several times until he could distinguish between these four rods. Finally he could name with a number every rod I held up individually.

I then took a piece of paper and wrote numerals from 1 to 10, for example:

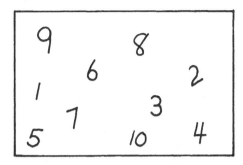

I told Eric to place *all* the rods (from a pile of rods) that are associated with a particular number over the numeral for that number on the paper; for example, *all* the yellow rods from the pile were to be placed on the numeral 5 on the paper.

Eric worked rapidly and with confidence until he had covered the paper with rods. All items were correct.

During this twenty-minute session Eric was attentive and grasped ideas rapidly. Apparently he had not realized previously that *every rod of a certain color is as long as every other rod of that same color.* Previously, he would always measure a rod with white rods before he would give a number name for that rod—no matter how many times he had used that particular color rod.

At the end of this session, it was apparent that, on sight of a particular rod, Eric knew its correct number name, for example, "eight" is the number name for *every* brown rod; "five" is the number name for *every* yellow rod, etc.

Geoboards: rows and columns
Logic

I
Work with geoboards

Each child was given a geoboard and three rubber bands (3 colors). Each board was numbered and lettered with chalk as follows:

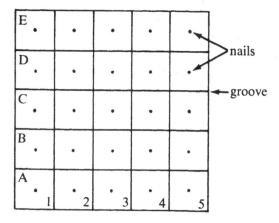

1   Lore: Place the geoboard upright with A and 1 closest to you. Across the geoboard, we have *rows*. The rows are marked by letters.

Push your finger over E row.

Push your finger over B row.

Push your finger over C row.

Put your light-brown rubber band over the nails across D row.

2   Lore: Up and down on the geoboard we have *columns*. The

columns are marked by numerals.
Push your finger over the nails in the 1 column.
Put your yellow rubber band over the nails in the 5 column.

3   Lore: How many nails are there on your geoboard?
    Children counted; answers given were 24, 25, 27, etc.; most
    children counted 25. Lore showed that there were 5 rows of
    5 nails each; five 5's are 25.

Lore demonstrated on the chalkboard how to identify (locate) points on the
geoboard.

1   Lore drew a large square of twenty-five smaller squares on the
    chalkboard to represent a geoboard.

2   Lore: I want my rubber band to go from E1 to A1.
    Children told her where to put rubber bands. As Lore drew
    this on the chalkboard, children placed their rubber bands on
    their individual geoboards:

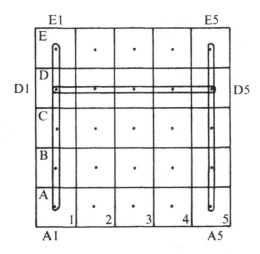

3   As Lore pointed to some positions on the geoboard, the children
    named the positions.

Lore	*Children*
What's this?	C3
What's this?	E2
What's this?	B4

4 Lore: Remove the rubber bands from your geoboards. I'll tell you what to find. Start at C1 and go to C5. With a rubber band, connect these two nails. Start at B5 and go to C1.

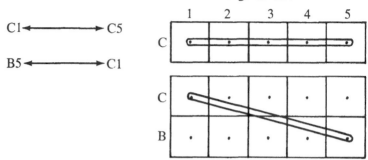

Children had difficulty following instructions: Lore checked each child's work, making corrections; she explained further what she wanted done. One child, Danny, very fast and accurate, helped other children at his table; other children whose work was correct were allowed to help those who had difficulty.

II
Geometric puzzles

Teacher showed the children a booklet of puzzle sheets, a sample of which is pictured below:

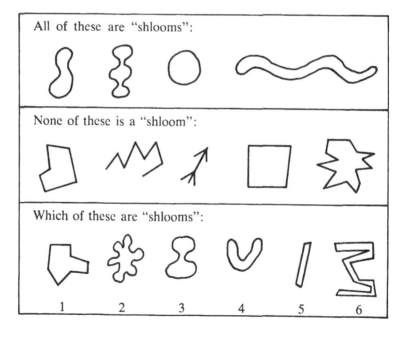

1 Children were able to identify the correct items (2, 3, 4) in the bottom portion of each sheet and give reasons for their choices.

Rodney: Shlooms are curvy.

Danny: Shlooms are all round.

2 Other pages followed in which other criteria, "have a string through a hole," "have some stripes," were the differentiating characteristics.

This sheet is not included in the Mathematics Laboratory Materials.

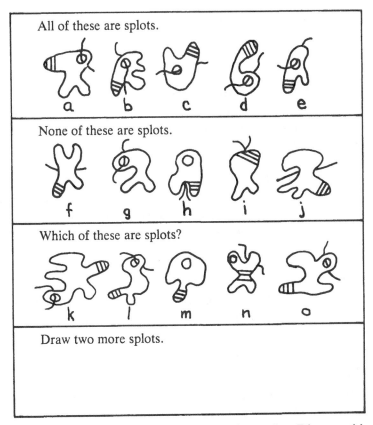

All of these are splots.

a b c d e

None of these are splots.

f g h i j

Which of these are splots?

k l m n o

Draw two more splots.

3 This kind of activity is good chalkboard exercise. Discuss with the children: "What are splots like?" "Why are f, g, h, i, j not splots?" "Why are k and l splots?"

Writing numerals
Difficult problems

I
Practice in writing numerals

Some children have had trouble in writing the numerals 9 and 6. Lore gave each child a small slip of paper. On one side of the paper, the numeral 9 was written; on the other side, the numeral 6.

1 Lore instructed the children to practice writing these numerals on the paper she had given them. She checked each child's work. When a child had difficulty, Lore gave him a demonstration in writing the numerals.

2 While most of the children were able to write the numerals, a few had difficulty, especially with writing the numeral 9. Usually numeral writing is *not* taught during the mathematics work period, but rather is included in other handwriting practice.

II
Problems that present difficulties

On the chalkboard, Lore wrote the following problems representing the types of problems that have been giving the children difficulty.

$\frac{1}{2} \times 6 = \square$ $6 + \square = 7$ $3 - \square = 2$ $3 + 3 = \square$

$4 \times 3 = \square$ $2 + \square = 4$ $5 - \square = 1$ $9 - 4 = \square$

                    $1 + \square = 1$ $4 - \square = 4$ $3 - 3 = \square$

                                                  $2 + 3 = \square$

Lore discussed each type of problem and explained, with the class participating, the meaning of each problem.

1 Two children, Gary and Louis, read the problems in the first group above.

They read $\frac{1}{2} \times 6$ as "one-half of six";

and read 4×3 as "four of the threes,"
or "four threes,"
or "four times three."

2 Some children had difficulty understanding the type of problem, $6 + \square = 7$. Lore explained that we want to find out what rod, when put end to end with the dark green rod (6) will be as long as the black rod (7).

$$6 + \square = 7$$

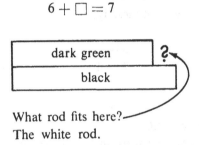

What rod fits here?
The white rod.

$$6 + \boxed{1} = 7$$

3 Peter had difficulty with his problem:

$$1 + \square = 1$$

Children explained that the 1 rod (white) plus the "zero rod" equals 1. One child came to the chalkboard and wrote "0" in the box.

$$1 + \boxed{0} = 1$$

4 Jeffrey had difficulty with this problem:

$$4 - \square = 4$$

Lore explained and demonstrated that if Jeffrey had the purple (4) rod in his hand to begin with, and wanted to end up with the purple rod, "zero" must be taken away:

$$4 - \boxed{0} = 4$$

5 Cliff read the problems in the fourth group, making a distinction between + and —. Often, children make errors reading the signs in problems. Instead of solving the problem $5 - 3 = \square$, for example, they might solve $5 + 3 = \square$.

III
Problem cards

Six children were given problem cards and were told to use the rods. The problems on each child's card were designed according to the type of problems which gave him trouble as evidenced by previous work in his folder. However, most of the problems were of these types:

$$3 + 5 = \square \qquad 5 - \square = 4$$
$$7 - 4 = \square \qquad 3 + \square = 10$$

IV
Written work

Children did written work in their individual folders.

V
Special work

Today I continued to work with Eric away from the rest of the group.

I wrote, one at a time, several numerals on the chalkboard. As I wrote a numeral, Eric found from a pile of different color rods the rod that corresponded to the numeral written. We played this game for about 5 minutes. Eric was fast and sure with his answers.

I then gave Eric a problem card like this:

$1 + 5$	$4 + 4$	$4 + 5$
$2 + 3$	$3 + 2$	$3 - 1$
$4 + 3$	$4 - 3$	$8 + 2$

I took the first problem $1 + 5$ and instructed Eric to place a 1 (white) rod end to end with a 5 (yellow) rod. He did this and immediately picked up a 6 (dark green) rod and measured his rod train $(1 + 5)$. I asked, "$1 + 5$ equals what?" "Six," answered Eric with great enthusiasm. I told Eric to do the rest of the *addition problems* on the card, and then I left the room. I returned about 5 minutes later. Eric had done all of the addition problems correctly. I then told him how to do the subtraction problems $(3 - 1; 4 - 3)$.

During the next five minutes I wrote problems on a sheet of paper. Eric worked each problem with rods and wrote the answer in the box $(4 + 2 = 6; 4 - 2 = 2;$ etc.$)$. Eric completed eight of these problems as I wrote them on the paper.

I knew that Eric could do simple addition and subtraction problems with the use of the rods. In discussions about the two sessions with this child, Lore and I decided to see if Eric would have the same success while working in the class with the other children.

The past month

]
Range of problems

The written work done by 18 first-graders during the past month involved problems in addition, subtraction, multiplication, fractions, and mixed operations with numbers 0 through 10. Eight of the children are multiplying and working with numbers greater than ten.

Samples of the types of problems the individual children can solve independently are listed below.

Eric:
$10 - 2 = \Box$
$7 - 6 = \Box$
$7 + 0 = \Box$
$2 + 2 - 1 + 1 = \Box$
$3 - 3 = \Box$
$4 + 3 = \Box$

Danny B.
$4 \times 3 = \Box$
$6 \times 4 = \Box$
$2 \times 3 + 2 \times 4 = \Box$
$\Box + \Box = 6$
$14 - \Box = 9$
$10 + 0 + 0 = \Box$
$5 + 5 + 1 + 1 = \Box$
$3 + 5 + 7 = \Box$

Audrey:
$5 - 4 + 7 = \Box$
$6 - 3 + 2 + 5 = \Box$
$3 + 3 - 2 + 2 = \Box$
$5 + \Box = 9$

Bobby:
$3 + 2 + 2 + 1 = \Box$
$6 - 6 = \Box$
$0 + 0 = \Box$
$5 + 5 = \Box$
$5 + \Box = 6$
$5 + \Box + 2 = 8$

Gary:
$13 - 9 = \Box$
$\frac{1}{8} \times 8 = \Box$
$5 + 5 + 5 + 5 = \Box$
$17 - 12 = \Box$
$2 + 4 + 6 = \Box$
$3 \times 4 = \Box$

Lynn:

$3 + 3 + 1 = \square$
$7 - 3 = \square$
$3 + 6 = \square$
$10 - 4 = \square$
$3 + 3 + 3 + 3 = \square$

Jeff:

$4 + 4 + 4 + 4 = \square$
$4 \times 4 = \square$
$3 + 4 + 4 = \square$
$7 - 2 - 1 = \square$
$7 - \square = 7$

Cliff:

$5 - 5 = \square$
$5 - \square = 3$
$5 + 2 + 2 = \square$

Fred:

$5 \times 3 = \square$
$6 + 4 - 7 - 3 = \square$
$6 - 3 + 5 = \square$
$3 + 2 + 6 = \square$

Peter:

$7 + \square = 9$
$10 - 5 = \square$
$6 - 6 = \square$
$0 + 0 = \square$
$3 - 3 = \square$
$5 + 5 = \square$

Ruthie:

$6 \times 2 = \square$
$3 \times 4 = \square$
$6 + 7 + 3 = \square$
$2 + \square = 8$
$6 - \square = 2$

Anne:

$4 \times 3 = \square$
$17 - 8 = \square$
$1 + 4 + 7 = \square$
$9 + 4 = \square$
$3 \times 7 = \square$

Danny S.

$1 + 2 + 3 + 4 = \square$
$10 - 10 = \square$
$4 + 4 = \square$
$5 - 4 = \square$

Louis:

$5 + 8 + 11 = \square$
$4 \times 9 = \square$
$15 - 9 = \square$
$3 \times 4 + 2 \times 3 = \square$
$\frac{1}{2} \times 28 = \square$
$4 \times 4 = 8 + \square$
$\square \times 3 = 9$
$0 = 12 - \square$
$1 + 2 + 3 + 4 + 9 + 1 + 10 = \square$

Ben:

$2 + 2 + 1 + 2 = \square$
$7 - 6 = \square$
$9 - 3 = \square$
$5 + 3 = \square$

David C.:

$40 - (2 \times 10) = \square$

$16 + (\frac{1}{2} \times 16) = \square$

$\square + 5 = 12$

$4 + 5 + 6 = \square$

$\frac{1}{2} \times 5 = \square$

$\frac{1}{2} \times 100 = \square$

$17 + 18 = \square$

David G.:

$5 + 2 + 1 = \square$

$4 + 0 = \square$

$9 - 9 = \square$

$3 + \square = 7$

$2 + 2 + 2 + 2 = \square$

$9 - 5 = \square$

Rodney:

$3 + 4 = \square$

$4 - 3 = \square$

$7 + 1 = \square$

$7 - 1 = \square$

$3 + 3 + 3 = \square$

$1 + 0 = \square$

Number line: addition and multiplication
Cuisenaire® rods: addition and subtraction

I
Number-line work

Lore invited the children to play the grasshopper game.

1 Children decided on a rule for grasshopper jumps on the number line.

Rule: □ ——→ □ + 2

"box goes to box plus two"
(The starting point is written in the box.)

2 The grasshopper, starting at 0, made a series of moves, landed at point 38 on the number line.

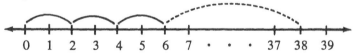

0 1 2 3 4 5 6 7 · · · 37 38 39

3 Lore: How many "+ 2" jumps did the grasshopper take?
Children: Nineteen. [They counted the jumps taken.]
Lore: When we start at 0 and land at 38, we move

19 × 2 or 38 units.

Lore: Suppose we had gone to point 40, how many "+ 2" jumps would we have had to take?
Children: Twenty "+ 2" jumps or 40 units.

95

II
Work with Cuisenaire® rods

Lore instructed the children to take three black (7), red (2), and yellow (5) rods, and make as many patterns for problems as they could.

1 Some of the problems children constructed were

$$5 + 2 = 7 \qquad 2 + 5 = 7 \qquad 7 = 2 + 5$$
$$7 - 2 = 5 \qquad 7 - \square = 5 \qquad 7 - 5 = 2$$

2 Lore hid four rods; she told the children how many rods she hid and how many colors. Children were to name the colors of the hidden rods.

How many rods (number)	(N) = 4
The sum of rods	(S) = 12
How many colors	(C) = 4

Gary determined that the rods were white (1), red (2), dark green (6), and light green (3):

$$1 + 2 + 6 + 3 = 12$$

Another possible solution was white (1), red (2), purple (4), and yellow (5):

$$1 + 2 + 4 + 5 = 12$$

Cuisenaire® rods: mixed operations

Ⅰ
Chalkboard demonstration

Lore introduced some "tricky" problems.

1 On the chalkboard she wrote:

$$4 \times 5 - 4 \times 3 = \square$$

Four of the 5's minus four of the 3's. With rods:

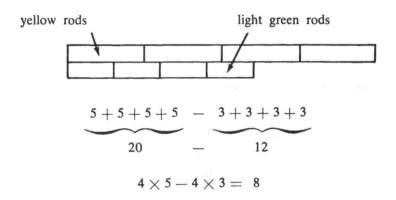

$$5 + 5 + 5 + 5 \quad - \quad 3 + 3 + 3 + 3$$

$$20 \quad - \quad 12$$

$$4 \times 5 - 4 \times 3 = \ 8$$

2 Next she wrote:

$$2 \times 4 + 2 \times 5 = \square$$

Two of the 4's plus two of the 5's, or

$$4 + 4 + 5 + 5 = \square$$

II
Written work
Children worked on lab sheets C1 through C12.

III
Directed play with rods
Lore asked the children to show her some rod patterns.

Number represented	Rod patterns
11	orange + white 10 + 1 black + lt. gr. + white 7 + 3 + 1 blue + red 9 + 2 (etc.)
14 (etc.)	orange + purple 10 + 4 (etc.)

IV
Negative numbers
Today Gary approached us with a discovery:

1 Gary: Bob, I just found out something.
Bob: What is it, Gary?
Gary: 10 − 10 = 0. Then 10 − 11 must be at least—0.

2 Bob: Let's see. Do you remember the grasshopper game with the number line? Let's draw a number line. Let's start at 10. Now count 11 (units) backward. [Gary counted on the number line.]

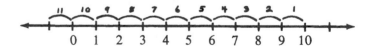

3 Bob: What do you call that point on the number line?

Gary: Uh, uh—one under zero.

Bob: What would you call the next point? [pointing to position of -2].

Gary: 2 under zero.

Bob: And the next?

Gary: 3 under zero.

Bob: So we have found out that $10 - 11 =$ what?

Gary: $10 - 11 =$ one under zero.

Comment: Although the teacher was not aware that any other children were listening, several days later Gary and a group of children were making number-line jumps into the region of the negative numbers and writing -1, -2, -3, as $0 - 1$, $0 - 2$, $0 - 3$.

Number line: odd and even

I
Number-line work

On the chalkboard a number line with numerals representing odd numbers only was drawn:

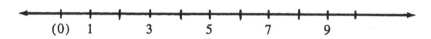

(0) 1   3   5   7   9

1 Lore: What numerals are missing?

One child, Danny B., quickly replied, "All the even numbers."

In answering the question: "What numerals are missing?" the child should have used the word *numeral*. Children, however, are not held responsible at this time for the correct phrasing. The teacher, of course, should be!

2 The children counted by 2's beginning with 1 up to 43 on the number line. They discovered that every stopping point represented an odd number.

The children observed that the last digit tells whether the number is even or odd. If, for example, the last digit (as in 553) is odd, the number is odd. 111,111,112 is an even number. 600,000,003 is an odd number.

II
Written work

The children were given lab sheet G3.

Rod patterns

I
Game: Lumberyard

Lore and a group of children were seated at a large table with a pile of rods.

1 Lore: [holding up a dark green rod (6) on top of a red rod (2)]
Let's pretend that we're working in a lumberyard. I am going
to pick up this much wood. You pick up as much wood as
I did.

Audrey picked up a yellow (5) rod and a purple (4) rod.
Other children disagreed. Audrey corrected herself. She picked
up a yellow (5) rod and a light green (3) rod:

dark green + red   yellow + light green
$$6 \quad + 2 = 8 \qquad 5 \quad + \quad 3 \quad = 8$$

2 Lore told the children to make their own piles of lumber, each
pile to include as much as Lore's pile (6 + 2). Some of the
patterns the children set up were:

$6 + 1 + 1$
$1 + 1 + 1 + 1 + 1 + 1 + 1 + 1$
$5 + 3$
$7 + 1$
$2 + 3 + 1 + 2$
$2 + 4 + 2$

One child, Ben, built the following patterns:

$$6 + 2 \qquad 6 + 1 + 1$$
$$5 + 1 + 2 \qquad 4 + 2 + 1 + 1$$
$$3 + 3 + 2 \qquad 2 + 2 + 2 + 1 + 1$$

II
Free play

The children played with a variety of materials that were in the room.

Numeral recognition: odd-even
Rod models: beginning use of parentheses

I
Odd-even

Today, the children continued to work on recognition of odd and even numbers.

1 Lore put numerals under the number line on the chalkboard. Children pointed to the even and odd numbers.

2 On a felt board with 100 squares, Lore placed a group of five "numeral" sponges. Lore asked, "What can I always do when a number is even?"
Children: You can put two things together.
Lore: Yes, even numbers have partners.

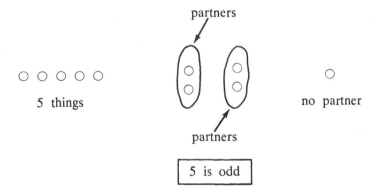

partners

○ ○ ○ ○ ○
5 things

partners

no partner

5 is odd

3 Children looked at each of the following groups to determine whether they could be paired off and told Lore whether each group consisted of an even or an odd number.

Other examples: number of windows; number of noses on face; number of toes on feet; number of eyes on face, etc.

II
Written work
Children worked on lab sheets B1 through B8.

III
Rod models
A group of four children showed Lore various ways of doing this problem:

$$4 + 2 + 2 + 2 = \Box$$

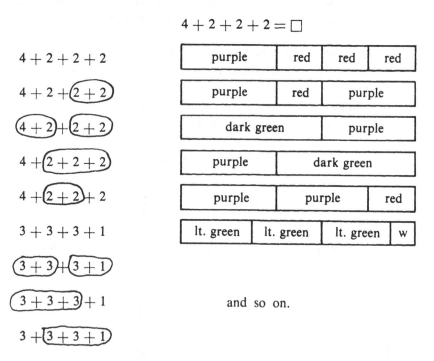

purple	red	red	red

$4 + 2 + 2 + 2$

purple	red	purple

$4 + 2 + (2 + 2)$

dark green	purple

$(4 + 2) + (2 + 2)$

purple	dark green

$4 + (2 + 2 + 2)$

purple	purple	red

$4 + (2 + 2) + 2$

lt. green	lt. green	lt. green	w

$3 + 3 + 3 + 1$

$(3 + 3) + (3 + 1)$

$(3 + 3 + 3) + 1$ and so on.

$3 + (3 + 3 + 1)$

Comment: The children thought this a very challenging game and used the problem as originally written only for "checking their answers."

104

November

Odd-even

I
Odd and even sets
Recognition of odd and even sets was continued.

1 A felt board and disk-shaped sponges were used in this group activity. On one side of the felt board, Lore placed a set of 5 sponges. On the other side, she placed a set of 4 sponges. Then she combined the two sets into one set of 9 sponges.

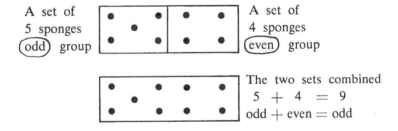

A set of
5 sponges
(odd) group

A set of
4 sponges
(even) group

The two sets combined
5 + 4 = 9
odd + even = odd

2 This activity with sets of sponges continued. The group determined that

$$odd + odd = even$$
$$odd + even = odd$$
$$even + odd = odd$$
$$even + even = even$$

See Section B, Odd-Even, in *Lab Sheet Annotations.*

Addition and subtraction

I
Written work

Two lab sheets, E30 and E31, were selected for the group. Some of the children used rods to prove their answers. Others worked without concrete materials. (See *Lab Sheet Annotations*, Section E, Addition and Subtraction.)

II
Free play

The children were free to use either the rods or geoboards and rubber bands.

Addition and subtraction

I

Game: Window cards

Lore used several special cards for practice in addition. The cards, as diagrammed below, are folded so that when one side, a "window," is open, a certain set of items (colored tape pasted on the inside of the card) can be seen. When the second window is open, another set of items is uncovered.

1 Lore held up a card, opening one window where 4 pieces of colored tape were exposed. The second window was kept closed.

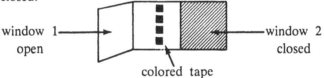

2 Window 1 was then closed and window 2 opened so that 3 pieces of tape were revealed.

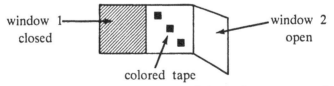

The children added: a group of four plus a group of three equals a group of seven.

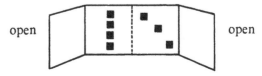

3 The window card game continued with a selection of cards which included the following sets of items:

a set of five / a set of two: $5 + 2 = 7$

a set of three / a set of six: $3 + 6 = 9$

a set of six / a set of five: $6 + 5 = 11$

II
Group activity:
Making window cards

The children enjoyed working with window cards and asked whether they could make some cards like them. They made several cards with oaktag sheets, plastic tape, and crayons. The children paired themselves; one child would "be the teacher" and hold up the window card for the second child, following the procedure described above.

Addition and subtraction

I
Writing problems

Lore showed the children how to write problems with use of the window cards. For example, when window 1 is open, three items are revealed; when window 2 is open, four items are revealed. The problem: $4 + 3 = \boxed{7}$ (a group of four plus a group of three equals a group of seven).

1 Lore showed the children how to use the window cards for subtraction problems:
Open both windows; a total group of 7 is revealed.

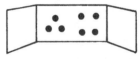

Close one window (for example, window 2); a group of 3 is revealed.

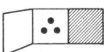

Problem:

$$7 - 4 = \boxed{3}$$

2 Children wrote on paper the problems which Lore demonstrated with window cards. Some of the problems are listed below.

$5 + 5 = \square$ $10 - 6 = \square$
$9 - 5 = \square$ $2 + 6 = \square$

Distinguishing numeral from number

I
Chalkboard work

Lore drew pictures on the chalkboard and asked questions about the pictures which the children answered.

Which is older?
The man (with beard).
Which is taller, a man or a baby?
A man, but the baby in the picture is taller than the man.

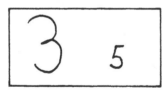

Which is taller?
The 3, but five is more than three.

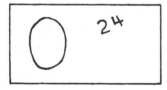

Which stands for more?
24!

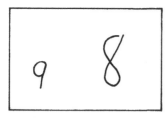

Cross out the numeral representing the bigger number.
A child crossed out the 9.

Cross out the numeral which stands for the smaller number of things.
A child crossed out numeral 4.
Put a circle around the numeral representing the bigger number *only if that numeral is a bigger picture.*
A child circled the 10.

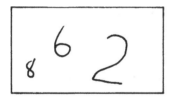

Erase the name for the smallest number in the box.
A child erased the 2.
Erase the name or numeral which stands for the largest number of things.
A child erased the 8.

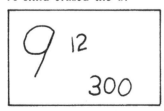

Erase the biggest picture.
A child erased the 9.
Erase the picture for the biggest number.
A child erased the 300.

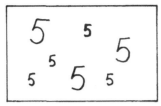

Erase the picture for the same number of things.
A child erased everything.

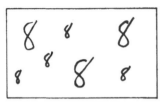

Erase pictures of (9 — 1) things.
A child erased everything.

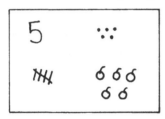

What does each stand for?
Five things.
What is only the name for five things?
5 and ┼┼┼.

Is this a number or a numeral?
A numeral.

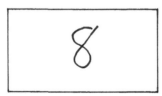

Is this a name or actually eight things?
A name.

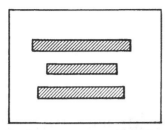

Is this a name or things?
Things.

Is this a name or things?
A name (for all girls called Ruthie).
(It is also a group of six letters and in this sense, we call it "things.")

Addition and subtraction

I
Diagnostic session

Can children do simple arithmetic problems without the use of rods? Before the children came into the classroom, I wrote the following on the chalkboard:

$$5 + \boxed{2} = 8 \qquad 3 + 5 = \boxed{9}$$
$$9 - \boxed{3} = 6 \qquad 3 + \boxed{1} - 7 = 10$$

1 When the children came into the classroom, I told them that someone had given me these problems to solve. The group was to decide whether I had done the work correctly.
Bob: Did I do all of my work correctly?
Children: No!
One by one the children came to the chalkboard and corrected the errors. I used demonstration rods to prove whether or not a child's solution was correct; only two children, Freddie and Cliff, made errors.

2 I wrote a series of problems on the chalkboard one by one; children came to the chalkboard and did the problems. No rods were used until a child had written his answer in the box. I asked the children how they could prove that the answers were correct; children told me what rods to use to prove answers correct.
Some problems were done without rods.

$$4 + \square = 9 \qquad 2 + \square + 3 = 7$$
$$6 + \square = 9 \qquad 3 + \square + 4 = 10$$
$$\square + 3 + 5 = 9$$

We learned that only five children appeared to have any difficulty in working problems without rods.

II
Written work
This lab sheet is not included in the Mathematics Laboratory Materials.

Name _____ Date_____

$7 - \square = 3$

$5 - 5 = \square$

$10 - \square = 4$

$6 + \square = 10$

$\square = 5 - 5$

$0 = 5 - \square$

$5 + 5 = \square$

$2 + \square + 3 = 9$

$7 - 7 = \square$

$3 - 3 = \triangle$

$6 - 4 = \bigcirc$

$5 + 3 + \square = 10$

$12 = 7 + \square + 2$

$3 + 3 + 2 + 2 = \square$

$$\begin{array}{r} 3 \\ 4 \\ +3 \\ \hline \end{array}$$

Fractions

I
Chalkboard work

The children, one by one, came to the chalkboard and drew lines dividing the circles and squares into halves, quarters, eighths, and thirds. They had no difficulty in handling the concept of fractions.

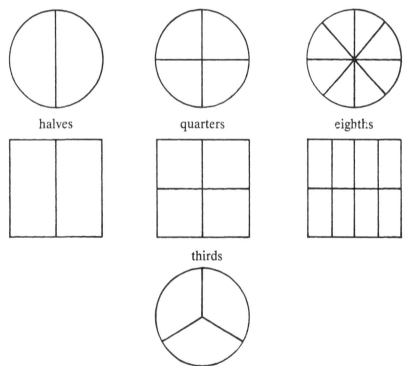

halves   quarters   eighths

thirds

Lore showed the children how to write fraction notation. She wrote ¼ in a section of one drawing and told the children that this means "one piece out of four pieces." The children labeled the other drawings: $\frac{1}{8}$, $\frac{1}{2}$, $\frac{1}{3}$, etc.

II
Written work
The children worked on lab sheet H4 and the lab sheet diagrammed below.

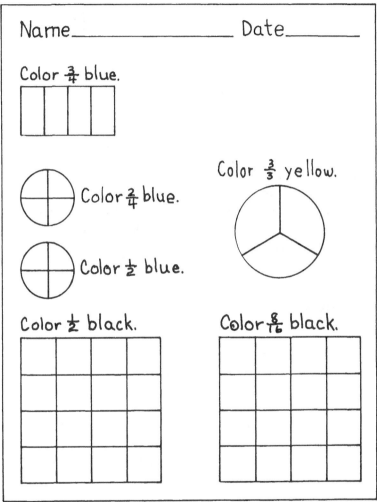

Name_____ Date_____

Color $\frac{3}{4}$ blue.

Color $\frac{2}{4}$ blue.

Color $\frac{3}{3}$ yellow.

Color $\frac{1}{2}$ blue.

Color $\frac{1}{2}$ black.

Color $\frac{8}{16}$ black.

This sheet is not included in the Mathematics Laboratory Materials.

See *Lab Sheet Annotations*, Section H, for additional lab sheets involving beginning work in fractions.

Much of the preliminary work in fractions occurred during free-play activities. For suggestions for preliminary work, see *Lab Sheet Annotations*.

Mixed operations
Work with fractions

I
Written work

On a table Lore laid out stacks of eight different lab sheets which covered simple operations in addition, subtraction, and multiplication. Children, in small groups, selected the sheets they wanted to do. Children were instructed to work without the use of Cuisenaire® rods.

II
Fractions

Each child was given a sheet of paper ($8\frac{1}{2}'' \times 11''$). Lore gave instructions.

1 Fold the paper in half.
Tear the paper where you have folded it.
Leave one of the halves just the way it is.
Tear the other one in half.
Now tear one of these sections in half.

As the children executed each step, Lore asked for the name of each piece. The children knew halves and quarters; some knew eighths.

2 On the chalkboard Lore drew diagrams representing the pieces of paper the children had torn. She labeled each drawing.

3 Then Lore told the children to put all the pieces together to see if they would fit into one big piece of paper.

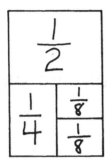

Addition and subtraction

I
Written work
The children did lab sheets E29 and E30. All except four children worked without the rods.

II
Free play
The children were allowed to play with the rods if they chose to do so. Many of the children asked for more lab sheets. Others made up their own problems.

Factoring

I
Rod game

After writing 15 on the chalkboard, Lore asked, "How can you show me this number in two rods?"

1 Children selected the orange (10) rod and the yellow (5) rod. Then Lore said, "Let the train of orange and yellow remain. Now can you make this length out of rods of the same color?"

2 The children answered Lore when she asked:

Can we make it out of	Children
10's (orange rods)?	No
8's (brown)?	No
6's (dark green)?	No
4's (purple)?	No
2's (red)?	No
9's (blue)?	No
7's (black)?	No
5's (yellow)?	Yes, three 5's
3's (light green)?	Yes, five 3's
1's (white)?	Yes, fifteen 1's

3 On the chalkboard, Lore wrote: $3 \times 5 = 15$; $5 \times 3 = 15$; and $15 \times 1 = 15$.

4 Lore asked the children to make rod patterns of 16 in as many ways as they could, using only one color rod in each line. The children found:

two 8's	$2 \times 8 = 16$
eight 2's	$8 \times 2 = 16$
four 4's	$4 \times 4 = 16$
sixteen 1's	$16 \times 1 = 16$

II
Written work

The children did lab sheets like the large one below. It is easy to make up other sheets for any number.

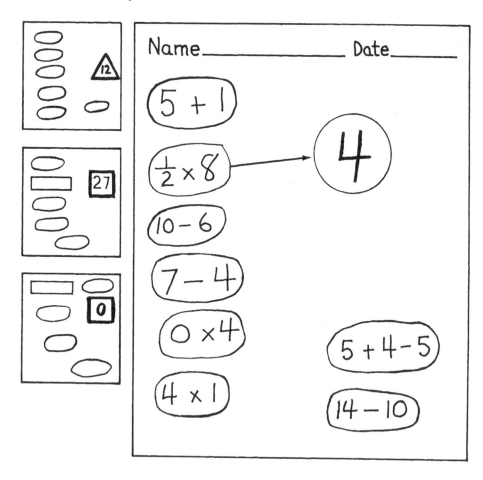

Number line
Fractions

I
Number-line game

Both Audrey and Freddie had birthdays in November. They decided to have a race on the number line.

1 The children decided on number-line rules for the race between Audrey and Freddie.

For Audrey, the "A" rule: $\Box \xrightarrow{A} \Box + 5$

"box goes to box plus 5"

For Freddie, the "F" rule: $\Box \xrightarrow{F} \Box + \Box$

"box goes to box plus box"

2 Both Freddie and Audrey started at point 1 on the number line:

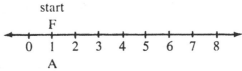

Here are the jumps they made:

Jump	Audrey $\Box \longrightarrow \Box + 5$	Freddie $\Box \longrightarrow \Box + \Box$
1st	$1 + 5 = 6$	$1 + 1 = 2$
2nd	$6 + 5 = 11$	$2 + 2 = 4$
3rd	$11 + 5 = 16$	$4 + 4 = 8$
4th	$16 + 5 = 21$	$8 + 8 = 16$
5th	$21 + 5 = 26$	$16 + 16 = 32$

3 The children determined that Freddie would always win the

125

race with his "doubling rule" if both he and Audrey started at the same point and continued to play the game for several jumps.

II
Written work

Lore gave each child a copy of lab sheet H34.

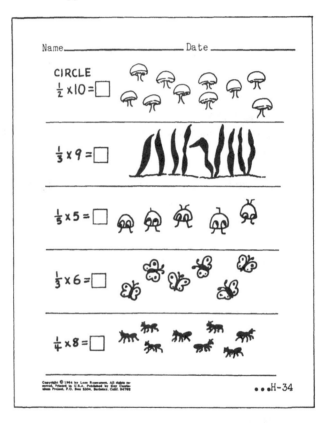

1 Lore read the first problem. Then she had the children tell her how to divide a group of ten things into two groups, each group containing the same number of things. On the chalkboard she drew 10 dots. A child drew the loops to divide the array into two groups of 5:

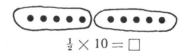

$$\tfrac{1}{2} \times 10 = \square$$

126

2 The children answered "yes" to each of the following questions: Did he use up the whole group (of ten things)? Did he get two groups? Are the same number of things in each of the two groups?

3 One child crossed out one of the groups of 5 dots and wrote "5" in the frame:

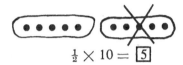

$$\tfrac{1}{2} \times 10 = \boxed{5}$$

4 Lore and the group followed the procedure described above to work the sheet.

Free play

I
Varied activities

The children selected materials they wanted to play with: toy money, three-dimensional puzzles, D-Stix, rods.

Addition
Work with rods

I
Dice game

Each child was given a paper plate containing a red die and a green die. On the chalkboard, Lore wrote the names of all the children. She asked Peter to come forward to help her demonstrate the game.

1 Lore gave these instructions, which Peter followed:
Shake up the dice in your (cupped) hands.
Drop the dice on the table.
How many dots are there on the face that shows (upright) on the red die? (3)
How many dots are there on the face that shows (upright) on the green die? (2)
How many dots altogether? (5)

2 Lore wrote the problem on the chalkboard, next to Peter's name:

$$\text{Peter} \quad \boxed{3} + \triangle\!\!\!2 = \bigcirc\!\!5$$

3 Using the procedure described above, the group played the game. Below are examples of the problems the children dictated to Lore to be written on the board.

$$6 + 6 = 12 \qquad 4 + 3 = 7 \qquad 6 + 3 = 9$$

129

II
Rod game
On the chalkboard Lore wrote a problem beside each child's name. Each child was asked to select the rods needed to build a model of the problem. Lore walked around to the tables to check the children's answers. Below are examples of the problems for which the children built rod models.

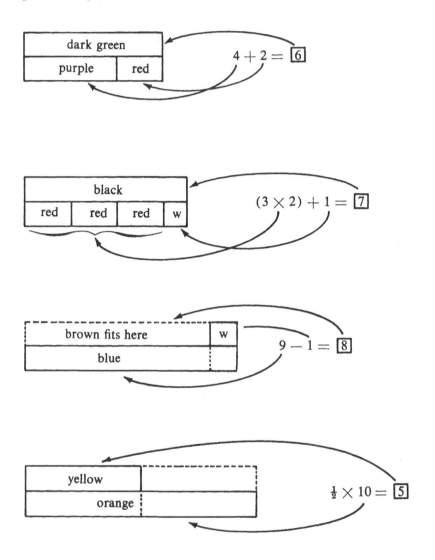

Mixed operations
Rod game

I
Written work

The children did lab sheet I15. They could use rods if they chose to do so. About one-half of the children worked on the problems without the use of rods.

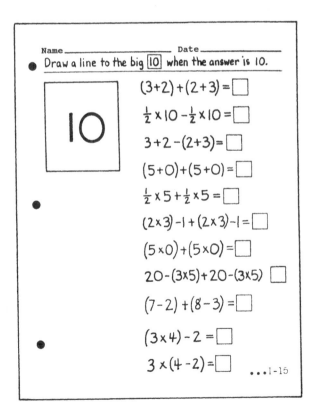

131

II
Putting away the rods

In order to get the rods put away in an orderly fashion, Lore played a game with the children.

1 Lore: Put into the box the rod that represents the following: $\frac{1}{2} \times 10$ (yellow); 2×5 (orange); $3 + 4$ (black); $\frac{1}{2} \times 4$ (red); 0 (the children picked up "air" as the "zero" rod); $0 + 1$ (white); $\frac{1}{2} \times 8$ (purple); $\frac{1}{3} \times 9$ (light green); $10 - 1$ (blue); $5 + 1$ (dark green).

2 Lore: On the chalkboard, write "tricky names" for the rod which we have not put away.

The brown rod had not been put away, so the children came to the chalkboard and wrote other names for 8.

$$4 + 4; \quad 1 + 1 + 1 + 1 + 1 + 1 + 1 + 1; \quad 7 + 1;$$

$$8 \times 1; \quad 5 + 3; \quad \tfrac{1}{2} \times 16; \quad 8 + 0$$

Rod patterns

I
Readiness work

On the chalkboard, Lore wrote the following problems. Then she said, "You need only three rods to do all of these problems: the light green (3), the purple (4), and the black (7)."

$$7 - 3 = \square \qquad 7 - \square = 4 \qquad 3 + 4 = \square$$

$$3 + \square = 7 \qquad 7 - 3 = \square \qquad 7 = 3 + \square$$

1 The children arranged this rod pattern on the table in front of them:

black	
purple	lt. gr.

2 Lore told the children to leave their patterns in front of them. Then as Lore called a child to the board, that child would read the problem aloud. Another child, from his seat, would then read the problem *with the answer*. The child at the board would write the correct answer in the frame.

3 A child would have little difficulty with a particular problem if he read it aloud, e.g., $7 - 3 = \square$ as "seven minus (take away) three equals *what?*" or $7 - \square = 4$ as "seven minus *what* equals 4?"

II
Written work

The children did a lab sheet about the number 8. They had little difficulty completing the work and asked for more sheets like E9. In the sample below, notice that one child made another rod pattern for the number 8 and wrote an entirely new set of problems.

Name __John D.__   Date __Nov. 23__

Use rods.

$5 + 3 = \boxed{8}$ $8 - \boxed{5} = 3$

$\boxed{8} = 3 + 5$ $\boxed{8} - 3 = 5$

$8 - 3 = \boxed{5}$ $8 - \boxed{8} = 5$

$\boxed{3} = 8 - 5$ $\boxed{3} - 5 = 3$

Make up some problems of your own.

$8 = 6 + 2$
$6 + 2 = 8$
$8 - 6 = 2$
$8 - 2 = 6$
$6 = 8 - 2$
$2 = 8 - 6$

• E – 9

The clock

I
"What time is it?"

On the chalkboard Lore put drawings of clocks (with no numerals, but with long and short hands). Children told her the time after noting the position of the hands and comparing the dial picture with the classroom clock directly above the chalkboard.

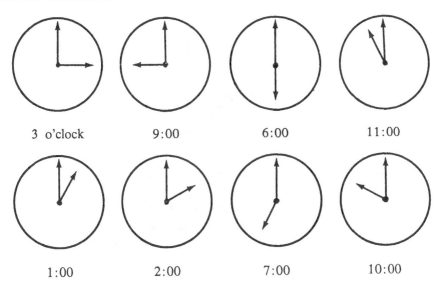

| 3 o'clock | 9:00 | 6:00 | 11:00 |

| 1:00 | 2:00 | 7:00 | 10:00 |

II
Written work

The children selected "clock" papers from Section X of the Mathematics Laboratory Materials.

Ratios
Place value

I
Directed play with rods

Lore told the children a story about a man who met some strange animals in the woods. She showed them a sample "animal" made out of rods.

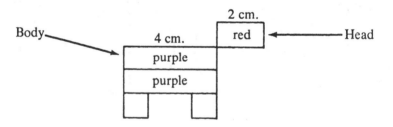

The body of the animal was twice the length of the head.

1   Each child was asked to make an animal like this and then to make other animals larger than the model shown, so that the body would be *twice the length of the head.*

2   The children made many such families of animals with rods, including some with a body as long as 40 centimeters and a head as long as 20 centimeters.

3   Lore asked the children to put all the rods they had used in a pile on their table. Now the children were asked to make animals with bodies *three times the length of the heads.* The chil-

dren worked quickly and with great interest. They built as many as 50 different models with the head-to-body ratio of ⅓:1.

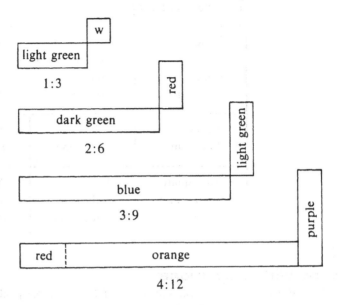

4 Lore asked the children to put their rods in a pile. The children said that they would like to build robots. Each robot should be made up of a *square body*, a *square head* (smaller than the body), and *legs* and *neck* that had the *same length as the side of the square head.*

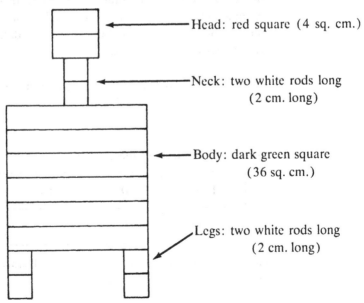

5 The children enjoyed building robots to the specification set. Below is the beginning of a chart that describes some of the robots the children built.

Head	Neck, legs	Body
white 1 sq. cm.	white 1 cm. long	light green 9 sq. cm.
yellow 25 sq. cm.	yellow 5 cm. long	blue 81 sq. cm.
Any square smaller than the body	As long as the side of the head	Any square larger than the head

II
Work with play money

Each child was given a random collection of 10 play-money bills. The denominations included were $1, $2, $5, $10, $20, $100, and $1,000. The child's job was to total the amount of money in his collection.

1 Lore wrote the name of each child on the chalkboard. When she called a particular child's name, the child would come to the board and write the total for each kind of bill he had. For example, Danny's collection contained 3 one-thousand-dollar bills, 5 one-hundred-dollar bills, and 2 ten-dollar bills. This is what he wrote on the board.

Danny: $3000   (thousands)
           $ 500
           $ 20

2 Lore made a chart on the chalkboard.

1000	100	10	1
3	5	2	0

How many one-thousand-dollar bills in Danny's collection?
How many one-hundred-dollar bills?

138

How many ten-dollar bills?
How many one-dollar bills?

3   Now Danny could get the total of his whole collection:

$$\begin{array}{r} \$3000 \\ 500 \\ 20 \\ \hline \$3520 \end{array}$$

4   The group followed the procedure described above. They were able to sort their bills according to denomination, total the amount in each denomination, and then total the amount in the whole collection.

Note: More of this kind of activity should have been included in the work of the group during the year.

The clock
Factoring

I
Work with the clock

On the chalkboard, Lore drew a picture of a clock without numerals.

1 The children were to come forward and place the small clock hand in the position of 5. They had no difficulty.

2 The small hand was erased and work continued for: 3:00; 7:00; 11:00; 1:00; 15:00.

Children were puzzled with 15:00. "How could there be a 15:00 on a clock where numbers are only up to twelve?"

After some moments of silence, one boy, Gary, went to the clock and placed the small hand in the 3 position. When questioned how he thought of putting it there, he said he counted three more places from the 12 position and he got to the 3 position because 12 plus 3 is 15.

Lore told the children that in Europe time is measured to 15:00, 20:00, and up to 24:00. 1:00 means 1:00 at night.

3 Lore: What then would be noon?
Children: 12:00.
Lore: What would be the time when you must go back to the buses because drivers are waiting for you in the afternoon?
Children: 15:00.
Lore: What time do most of you eat supper?
Children: 18:00. [Only two children said this.]
Lore: Will you be up when it is 7:00 on this clock?

Children: Yes. [Most felt this to be true because they were up at 7:00 in the morning.]

Lore: Would you be sleeping or awake when it is 20:00?

Children recognized that it would be 8:00 at night, as they usually figure it, and that it would be their bedtime.

II
Factoring using Cuisenaire® rods

Each child was given three orange rods and asked to build a train. Lore asked, "If the white one is our unit, how long will a train of three orange rods be?"

The children quickly answered 30. (One child said it would be 30 cm. long because each white rod is 1 cm. long.)

1 Lore: Rebuild a train of that length in one color, but use a color different from orange. In what colors do you think we can do it?

The children suggested red, yellow, dark green, white, light green, purple.

2 Lore wrote the suggestions on the chalkboard and children tried out each one. The purple was erased because children found that they couldn't make length 30 in groups of 4.

3 One child was puzzled and asked why it could not be done in groups of 4 if it could be done in groups of 2.

4 Children were asked how many 2's, 5's, 6's, 3's they needed in order to make length 30. Lore wrote each equation on the chalkboard.

five 6's	or	$5 \times 6 = 30$
six 5's	or	$6 \times 5 = 30$
		$3 \times 10 = 30$
		$10 \times 3 = 30$
		$1 \times 30 = 30$ [One child said this although we did not have a 30 rod.]
		$30 \times 1 = 30$
		$15 \times 2 = 30$
		$2 \times 15 = 30$

141

5 Lore asked the children how many "zero rods" equal 30. Guesses varied from "at least 100" to "one-thousand million" to "30" until Lore asked, "Is 30 $\times$ 0 thirty?" The children responded, "No."
"Is 100 $\times$ 0 thirty?"
"No."
Then a comment was made: "We'll never be able to make 30 out of zero rods alone!"

6 Children volunteered to hide their faces as class members asked, without having any models or looking at the chalkboard, how many 5's equal 30; how many 2's equal thirty; how many 6's equal thirty; etc.?

III
Work with geoboards

Geoboards were taken out. Lore said, "With one rubber band, make a triangle—any size, any shape triangle. How many sides does a triangle have?" The children answered, "Three."

1 Lore: Make a rectangle. (The word "rectangle" was often used by the teacher.) How many sides does a *rectangle* have? Children: Four.

2 Lore: Make a 5-sided figure. Make sure it has 5 sides. Such a figure is called a *pentagon*. [This is a new word for the children. Lore wrote "pentagon" on the chalkboard.]
The children continued the lesson, engaging in free play with geoboards.

IV
Practice in multiplication

Before they left, five children were taken aside, one at a time, and given a multiplication oral-dictation test.

1 Except for one or two hesitations, all five of the children tested immediately responded to the multiplication facts on the sheet.

2 As a result of their experiences with the rods, the children became very certain that multiplication was always commutative. (The word "commutative" was not used.) Once they knew, therefore, what 3×5 was, they knew immediately what 5×3 was. This knowledge was developed, for example, through building a rectangle with three 5 rods, and then a congruent rectangle of five 3 rods on top of the first.

5 light green rods

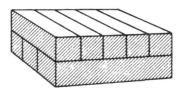

3 yellow rods

Lab sheets F13 and F14 provide work on the commutative property of addition.

December

Arithmetic operations
Clock arithmetic
Place value
Progressions
Odd-even
Number line

Clocks
Computation

I
Written work

The children were given lab sheets X1 and X2. On the chalkboard Lore drew a picture of the first two clocks shown on X1. One child wrote 9:00 underneath the picture of the first clock. Another child drew in the long and short hands on the second clock to show 2:00. Then the children worked individually on the two sheets.

II
Dictation of problems

After the children had completed their written work and papers had been collected, Lore dictated some problems. The purposes of this activity were (a) to see whether the children could write problems from dictation without confusing operational symbols or omitting symbols, and (b) to see if they could handle the computation involved in the problems without using rods.

Following are the problems Lore dictated. On a piece of plain paper, each child wrote the problems and supplied the answers in the frames. The children had no trouble with these problems. One child wrote $3 \times 5 = 10$ instead of $3 \times 5 = 15$. Lore corrected him by having him reread the problem (which he had read as $2 \times 5 = \square$).

$$3 + 5 = \square$$ "3 plus 5 equals what?"
$$8 - 3 = \square$$ "8 minus 3 equals what?"
$$2 \times 4 = \square$$ "2 times 4 equal what?"
  "2 of the 4's equal what?"
$$9 - 4 = \square$$
$$3 \times 5 = \square$$
$$4 - 4 = \square$$

III
Make up your own problems

On the back of the piece of paper on which the children had written the problems that Lore dictated, each child made up his own problems. "These are problems for you to solve, Lore," one child said.

1 Lore went from child to child, looking at the problems that each child had made up, solving a problem that was made up "for Lore," writing interesting problems on the chalkboard for the whole group to try, encouraging individual children to solve the problems they had made up.

2 Some of the problems made up by the children and solved by the group were:

Eric	Danny
$9 \times 8 = \square$	$3 \times 8 - 4 = \square$

Anne
$$10 + 10 + 10 + 10 + 3 + 5 = \square$$

The children enjoyed whispering the answers to Lore. More than half the group answered "48" to Anne's problem.

3 Anne presented another problem for the group to solve:

$$10 - 18 = \square$$

Lore: I think Anne really meant a different problem.
Gary: Anne meant $18 - 10 = \square$. $10 - 18$ is on the other side of 0.
Louis: Yes, $10 - 18 = 8$ on the other side of 0.

Clocks
Place value

I
The correct time

The children, in turn, came to the chalkboard and "corrected the time" on the pictures of the clocks Lore had drawn.

Lore's drawings   Child's correction

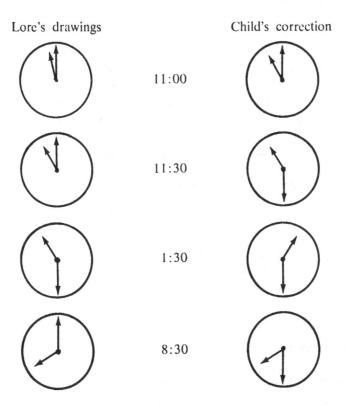

149

II
Writing large numbers

Before this group session, Lore had made a set of place-value blocks (base 10) out of some Cuisenaire® rods. In one pile on a table at the front of the room she had approximately 15 white rods. In another pile she had 12 orange rods. By taping together 10 orange rods, she had made an orange square. Ten orange squares were taped together to make a block.

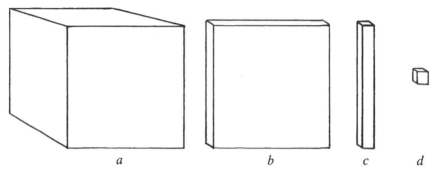

a	*b*	*c*	*d*

1 Lore: If we call *d* our unit or our 1, then what is *c*?
Child: 10.
Child: 10 of *d*.

2 By using rods to measure the concrete materials which Lore had made, the children proved that *b* = 100 (ten of the 10's); *a* = 1000 (ten of the 100's). The children called *a* the "ten-hundred rod." Lore suggested another name, "one thousand."

3 Lore drew a chart on the chalkboard:

1000	100	10	1

Then she said, "We are going to use this chart in a game we are going to play. It is like the chart that is on the lab sheet I am going to give you."

III
Written work

Lore gave each child a sheet like the one diagrammed below. This sheet is not included in the Mathematics Laboratory Materials. See Section M, Place Value, in *Lab Sheet Annotations*, and lab sheets M1 through M5.

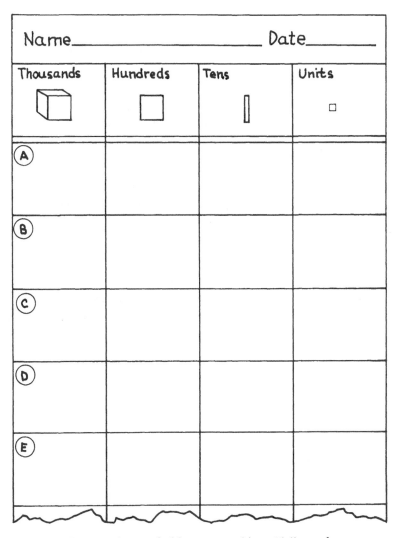

Thousands	Hundreds	Tens	Units
Ⓐ			
Ⓑ			
Ⓒ			
Ⓓ			
Ⓔ			

Name_____ Date_____

1 Lore: I am going to hold up something. Tell me how many thin₃s I am holding up. Someone come to the chalkboard and write the number of that kind of thing under the right picture.

Lore held up   Child wrote

1000	100	10	1

two 100 rods ——→ 2 3 4

three 10 rods ——

four 1 rods ——

2 Following this procedure, the group wrote other large numbers: 300 (three of the 100's, no 10's, no 1's); 1452 (one 1000 rod, four 100 rods, five 10 rods, two 1 rods).

3 Then Lore held up various collections of rods and the children, at their seats, wrote the corresponding numerals on their lab sheets. When the sheet was completed, Lore helped the children read what they had written:

> 234 is read "two hundred thirty-four."
> 300 is read "three hundred."
> 1452 is read "one thousand, four hundred, fifty-two."

IV
Free play

Following the completion of the activities described above, the children were allowed a 10-minute free-play period. Many of the children built with the rods. Others continued to make up clock problems and problems about place value.

Addition and subtraction
Number line

I
Number-line puzzles

Lore used the number-line strip (adding-machine tape marked off in units three inches apart) tacked across the top of the chalkboard. She labeled the points.

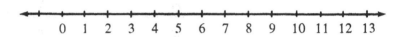

0 1 2 3 4 5 6 7 8 9 10 11 12 13

1 Lore: I am going to give you a puzzle problem. You can use the number line to solve the problem.

On the chalkboard she wrote

6 ———➤ 9

Lore: You must decide what numeral, representing a certain number of jumps, should be written above the arrow.

The children made guesses. Many of them said three. They proved it on the number line:

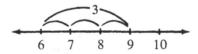

6 7 8 9 10

'3' should be written above the arrow:

jump
3
6 ———➤ 9
start   stop

153

2 Lore: What does this mean?

Children: Start at 9. Jump back to 6.
Lore: How big is the jump?
Children: Three.

jump
3
6 ◄———— 9
stop   start

3 Lore presented several of these problems and the children determined the size of the jump, or the starting point, or the stopping point. Sometimes they used the number line to prove their answers. Many of the children solved the problems without the use of the number line, for when they understood the idea, they were able to compute mentally.

"How big is the jump" problems:

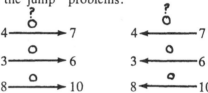

"Where did I start" problems:

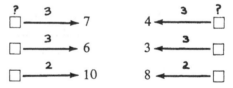

"Where did I stop" problems:

4 ——3——► ? □   ? □ ◄——3—— 7
3 ——3——► □   □ ◄——3—— 6
8 ——2——► □   □ ◄——2—— 10

II
Written work
The children were given copies of lab sheet E18. (See also lab sheets E19, E20.)

Addition, subtraction, and multiplication

I
Chalkboard game

Lore drew a diagram on the chalkboard. The children volunteered to come up and draw a line from each problem where the answer was 10, and to cross out those problems where the answer was not 10.

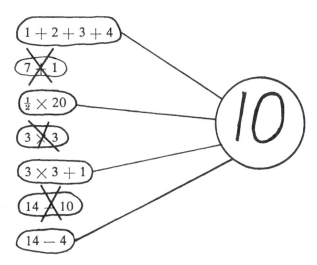

Then Lore asked the children to think of other "tricky ways" of writing 10. The children made up their own problems, some of which are listed below, and wrote them on the chalkboard.

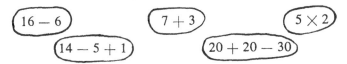

II
Number-line problems

Lore wrote the following problems on the chalkboard. The children came up and put the answers in the frames. They proved their answers by using the number line.

$$6 \xrightarrow{\text{4}} \square \qquad 4 \xrightarrow{\text{6}} \square$$

$$\square \xleftarrow{\text{4}} 10 \qquad 7 \xrightarrow{\text{O}} 12$$

Now the children were ready for their written work.

III
Written work

The children were given lab sheets E19 and E20, and another sheet on which they were to write into loops "tricky names" for 12.

Addition, subtraction, and multiplication

I
Chalkboard work

The children came to the chalkboard and drew lines from the problems where the answer was 15 to the big 15. They crossed out problems where the answer was not 15.

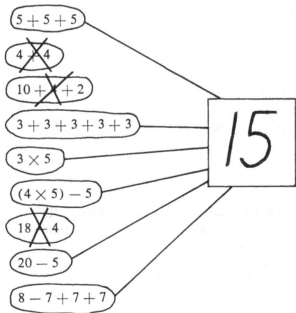

II
Written work

The children selected sheets from Section E, Addition and Subtraction, and from Section F, Multiplication.

Clocks
Addition, subtraction, and
multiplication

I
What time is it?

Lore drew the long hand on a picture of the clock on the chalkboard. One child drew in the short hand; another child wrote the time notation representing the time shown on the clock picture.

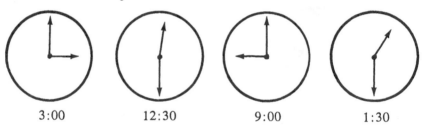

| 3:00 | 12:30 | 9:00 | 1:30 |

II
Tricky ways of saying and writing "0"

The children came to the chalkboard and drew lines from the problems where the answer was 0 to the big 0 in the frame.

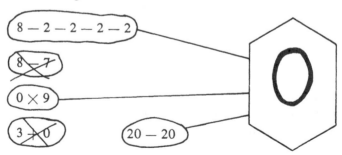

The children then made up their own names for 0.

$$\boxed{5 - 4 - 1} \qquad \boxed{0 - 0} \qquad \boxed{4 + 0 - 0 - 4} \quad \text{etc.}$$

III
Written work

Several lab sheets from Sections E, F, and G were laid out on a table. Each child selected three sheets to work on for approximately 20 minutes.

Progressions
Addition and subtraction
Odd-even

I
From point to point

On the chalkboard Lore drew a series of points. The children were asked to come forward and "make a road" from each point to every other point in a particular group of points. The "roads" had to be straight lines.

1 Three points

Number of lines: 3

2 Four points

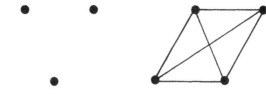

Number of lines: 6

3 Five points

Number of lines: 10

The children responded enthusiastically.

II
Five-minute quiz
Lore gave each child a copy of lab sheet E26. None of the children used rods to solve the problems.

III
Number-line work
Lore drew a number line on the chalkboard. She labeled a point "1" in red chalk, the next point "2" in white chalk. The children, in turn, came forward and labeled the other points, the odd numbers in red, the even numbers in white.

1 The children observed that 0 must be an even number because 1 is odd, 1 "on the other side of zero" is odd; all even numbers fall between two odd numbers. Since 0 falls between two odd numbers, then 0 must be an even number.

2 Most of the children seemed to be familiar with negative numbers and could label the number line to −10, −11, −12, etc.

3 The children understood that with a number-line rule such as □ ──────▶ □ − 2 (box goes to box minus 2), the stopping point would always be an *odd* number if "we start on an *odd* number." If "we start on an *even* number," the stopping point will always be an *even* number.

4 The children came to the front of the room and used this number-line rule, starting first with an odd number, and then with an even number.

Rule: □ ⟶ □ − 2

Odd

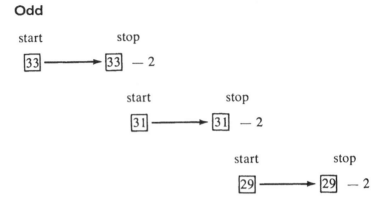

start   stop

|33| ⟶ |33| − 2

       start   stop

      |31| ⟶ |31| − 2

              start   stop

             |29| ⟶ |29| − 2

Even

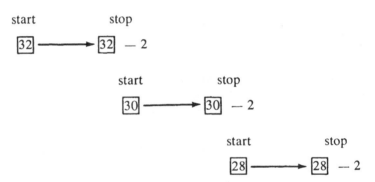

start   stop

|32| ⟶ |32| − 2

       start   stop

      |30| ⟶ |30| − 2

              start   stop

             |28| ⟶ |28| − 2

See Section N, Number Lines and Functions, in *Lab Sheet Annotations*.

January

Summary of Topics

Arithmetic operations
Factoring
Series and progressions (geometry)
Odd-even
Clock arithmetic
Money problems
Oral work
Series and progressions
Doubling
Fractions
Squares
Triangle numbers
Equalities and inequalities
Symbols
Geometric recognition

Addition, subtraction, and multiplication

I
Written work and free play with rods

Lab sheets G5 and G6 were given out. Some children did both sheets but others completed only one. Half the class worked without rods.

Boxes of rods were on each table. Children had 10 minutes of free play.

II
Factoring game using rods

1 Lore: Pretend that each rod represents a certain amount of money (the white rod = $1; red rod $2, and so on). I'll say, "I want $15 in 3 rods of the same color. What would you bring to me?"

Children: Three yellow (5) rods.

2 As the game proceeded, Lore asked for the following "amounts":

$12 in four rods of the same color
$12 in three rods of the same color
$20 in five rods of the same color
$16 in two rods of the same color
$ 9 in three rods of the same color

3 This game could be played again using a different code. Let the red rod stand for $1.00. Then what rod equals $.50? What rod equals $2.00? And so on. Or, if the orange rod equals $1.00, then the white rod equals □.

Multiplication
Series and progressions

1
What is missing?

Lore wrote several problems on the chalkboard. The children placed the correct numerals in the frames.

$3 + 3 =$ ⑥

$3 +$ ③ $+$ ③ $= 9$

$3 + 3 +$ ③ $+$ ③ $= 12$

$3 + 3 + 3 + 3 + 3 =$ ⑮

$3 + 3 + 3 + 3 + 3 + 3 =$ ⑱

$3 + 3 + 3 + 3 + 3 + 3 + 3 + 3 =$ ㉔

1 Lore suggested that the last problem could be written a shorter way. On the chalkboard one child wrote $8 \times 3 =$ 24 . The child said that we know that $6 \times 3 = 18$ and that $2 \times 3 = 6$. So $8 \times 3 = 24$ because:

$$
\begin{array}{ll}
18 & \text{(six 3's)} \\
+\ 6 & \text{(two 3's)} \\
\hline
24 & \text{(eight 3's)}
\end{array}
$$

2 On the number line, Lore illustrated this problem:

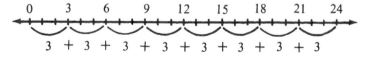

$$
\begin{array}{ccccccccc}
0 & 3 & 6 & 9 & 12 & 15 & 18 & 21 & 24
\end{array}
$$

$$3 + 3 + 3 + 3 + 3 + 3 + 3 + 3$$

II
Oral drill

Lore asked several children, one at a time, to turn their backs to the chalkboard. Then she asked, "Three times three equals what?" "Three times two equals what?" Then Lore said to the children, "Turn around and show us where, on the chalkboard, you saw four 3's." A child pointed to $3 + 3 + 3 + 3 = 12$.

III
Written work

Before giving the children lab sheets about points and lines, Lore drew three points on the chalkboard. She asked Ruthie to connect the points in all possible ways, or "build roads from point to point."

1   Ruthie did this:

Lore asked, "How many lines?" The children replied, "Three."

2   Lore then gave the children rulers, lab sheets, and pencils. She explained what was to be done. (These lab sheets, with groups of dots like those illustrated below, can be made up by the teacher. In Level 5 of the pupil materials are two sheets [U11, U12] that are similar to the sheets used in this group session.)

3   Several children connected four points like this:

   4 lines

Lore showed that there are two other possibilities:

   6 lines

4   Only one child had real difficulty in following the instructions. Lore worked with him individually and his work improved on the second sheet.

167

Another child worked very carefully on the items showing 5 and 6 points. She was very logical in her approach. She drew the outside lines first. Then she put a finger on each point, one at a time, and drew all of the "roads" she could before taking another point and doing the same thing. Lore cited this child's work and suggested that other children might find this approach useful.

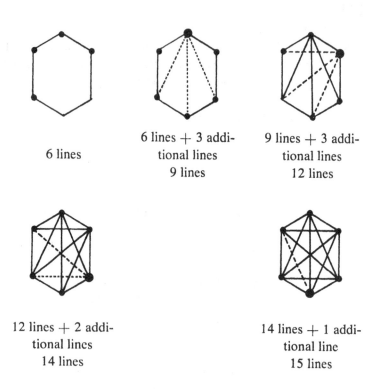

6 lines

6 lines + 3 additional lines
9 lines

9 lines + 3 additional lines
12 lines

12 lines + 2 additional lines
14 lines

14 lines + 1 additional line
15 lines

Read Section U, Series and Progressions, in *Lab Sheet Annotations.*

Odd-even
Clock arithmetic
Money problems

I
Written work

Lore's analysis of the children's past written work was a basis for her dividing the class into two groups. One of the groups (about half the class) had shown great proficiency in solving problems in addition, subtraction, multiplication, fractions, and mixed operations. The other group had shown less proficiency in their written work and still needed to use model-making materials in solving the more difficult problems.

1   Displayed on one table were lab sheets from which the children in the more proficient group could choose. On another table were sheets from which the second half of the class could choose. Many of the available lab sheets were copies of sheets already done by the children during the past several weeks. Some of the sheets were new to the children.

2   Most of the lab sheets were selected from C, Addition; E, Addition and Subtraction; F, Multiplication; G, Addition, Subtraction, and Multiplication; and H, Fractions.

3   The children worked for 20 minutes on the sheets they had chosen. It was surprising to note that only a few children needed rods to solve most of the problems on the sheets. When rods were used, they served as a checking device. Usually a child had made a guess and then built a model to prove his answer.

169

II
Chalkboard work

Lore told the children to raise their hands when the number of items put on the chalkboard was *even*. If the number of items was *odd*, hands were to be kept down.

1 One by one, Lore drew the following groupings on the chalkboard. The children responded by raising their hands, or keeping their hands down.

Grouping	Response
• • • •	hands up (even)
• • • • • • •	hands down (odd)
= // ⁒ =	hands up (even)

2 The children determined when a particular grouping was even or odd by putting loops around pairs of items. If an item was left without a "partner," the child knew that the particular grouping was odd.

III
What time is it?

Lore drew three sets of "clock" hands. The children told her the time represented.

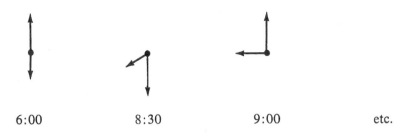

| 6:00 | 8:30 | 9:00 | etc. |

Then Lore reminded the children that European clocks go to 24:00. She asked, "What are you doing at 24:00?" The children responded, "Sleeping. That's midnight." "What are you doing at 7:00?" (Eating breakfast) "What are you doing at 15:00?" (Going home on the bus)

IV
Clock game

One child was asked to leave the room. An object was hidden (given to another child). The child who left the room returned and was told that he was at 12 on the clock. The object was hidden at 9:00. The child was to determine where 9 would be in relation to his own position. He then went to the child who was seated approximately at the position of 9. And that's where the object was hidden.

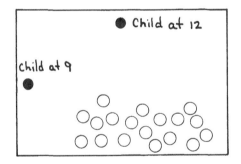

V
Which would you rather have?

Lore asked the children, "Which would you rather have?"

$1.00 or 100¢?   (Either, because $1.00 and 100¢ are the same amount.)
($1.00 because I don't want all of those pennies.)

½ dollar or 2 quarters?   (It doesn't matter because ½ dollar = 50¢ and 2 quarters = 50¢.)

2 dimes or 3 nickels?   (2 dimes because 2 dimes = 20¢ whereas
                            3 nickels = only 15¢.)

Lore said, "I had 103 pennies, but dropped all of them on the floor. I found only 98 of them. How many were still lost?" The children determined that 5 were still lost because

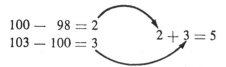

$$100 - 98 = 2$$
$$103 - 100 = 3$$
$$2 + 3 = 5$$

Doubling and halving

I
Written work

Bob gave each child a copy of lab sheet E32, and a copy of another sheet (not included in the Mathematics Laboratory Materials). The children quickly realized what was to be done and proceeded to work.

(See lab sheets F23–F26 in Level 3 for work in doubling and halving.)

The observations that the children made regarding lab sheet E32 were that (a) all the answers in the doubling exercise at the top of the page were even numbers, and (b) that the double of a particular number is always two more than the double of the preceding number. For example, the double of 4 $(4 + 4 = 8)$ is 2 more than the double of 3 $(3 + 3 = 6)$.

Fractions

I
Readiness work
For certain children the words listed below were placed on the chalkboard. As each word was written, the children would pronounce it. Then the meanings of the words were discussed.

big   bag   is   wag   wig   fit

II
Written work
The Snowman booklet (H7–H13) was given to each child. The children were divided into three groups according to their reading skills so that the children who needed help were seated at one table, those who needed no help were seated together, and those who needed just a little help were seated at still another table. All the children had the same booklet.

The children had little difficulty with the arithmetic in the booklets, and they thoroughly enjoyed the work. Most of the children asked for a second booklet to take home.

Multiplication
Fractions

I
Written work

The children were free to select lab sheets from Section H, Fractions, and Section F, Multiplication. They worked quietly and competently.

Series and progressions
Fractions

I
Continuing the series

Lore wrote several series on the chalkboard. The children were to determine the pattern and continue the series.

(1, 2); (2, 4); (4, 8); (8,); (,); (,)
(2, 1); (4, 2); (6,); (,); (,); (,)

The children were able to do the problems listed above, but they had trouble with this one:

(1, 3); (2, 6); (3,); (,)

Lore used rods in pairs—white rod, light green rod (1, 3); red rod, dark green rod (2, 6); etc. The children determined that the larger rod in these pairs was always three times the smaller rod. They decided that 9 should be paired with 3; the third pair of rods would be a light green and a blue.

II
Written work

Lore gave each child a copy of the Children's booklet (H17–H23). Lore helped those who needed assistance.

Mixed operations
Squares

I
Written work
Several lab sheets similar to E21, E36, and G3 were laid out on a table.
The children selected one or more of the sheets and worked for 20 minutes.

II
What is a square?
Lore had sorted the white rods out of the collection of Cuisenaire® rods, and
small boxes containing several white rods were placed on each table. The
children were asked to stamp the fleshy part of their hands with one side
of a white cube. They identified the shape of the impression as a square.

With white cubes, the children built the following squares:

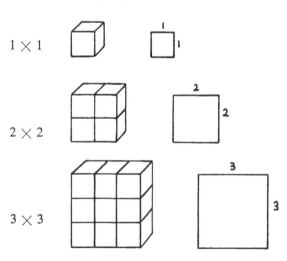

1×1

2×2

3×3

4 × 4

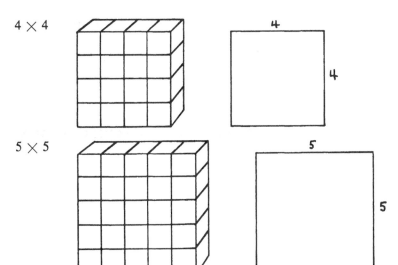

5 × 5

Series and progressions

I
Triangle numbers

Lore used white cubes from the rod collection to demonstrate the building of the triangle numbers. She used three white rods.

Then she asked Peter to make a three-layered triangle using more than three white rods. Peter built this:

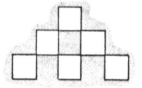

1 With white cubes the children continued to build models of the triangle numbers. With three rods they built a two-layered tower as shown above. With six rods they built a three-layered tower; with ten rods a four-layered tower, and so on.

Lore asked, "What kind of numbers should we call these?" The children said that they should be called *triangle* numbers because the basic shape of each tower is a triangle.

2 On the chalkboard Lore drew pictures of the triangle patterns.

She labeled each diagram:

A   B   C   D

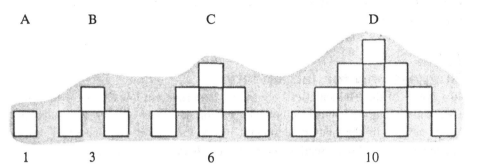

1   3   6   10

Then she asked the children, "What numbers would I have to add up in each pattern?" The children answered as follows:

in A, 1
in B, 1 + 2
in C, 1 + 2 + 3
in D, 1 + 2 + 3 + 4
then, 1 + 2 + 3 + 4 + 5

Danny said that he knew that the next pattern would total 21 ones because 15 + 6 = 21 [1 + 2 + 3 + 4 + 5 + 6 = 21]

II
Square numbers

From the triangle patterns built by the children, the square patterns were built. Lore said, "Add something else to each triangle to make a square."

Triangle   Square
3   add 1   4

Triangle   Square
6   add 3   9

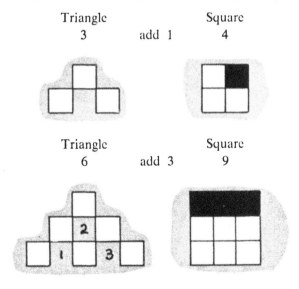

181

The following observation can be made: The number of additional squares needed to build the next square number is the number of the "holes" in the triangle patterns.

III
Suggestions for lab sheets
In Level 4 of the Mathematics Laboratory Materials are lab sheets on squaring (Section P) and on triangle numbers (Section U). The teacher can make up sheets similar to the ones diagrammed below for use at the first-grade level. The teacher should read Sections P and U in *Lab Sheet Annotations*.

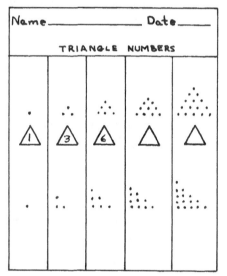

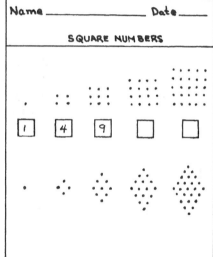

Squares

I
Follow-up of a child's observation

One child (Danny B.) observed at a glance that a small tray of cubes contained 100 cubes. Lore asked, "How did you know this so quickly?" Danny said, "Because there are 10 [cubes] across the top and 10 down, and $10 \times 10 = 100$."

1 Lore drew a diagram on the chalkboard:

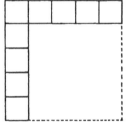

She said, "Suppose I fill in all of this space. How many [little squares] will I have then?" The children made guesses. Six children said 25. Lore proved that these children were correct; she filled in the space as in the diagram below. The children counted the squares. The total was 25.

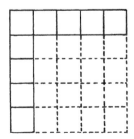

Then Lore wrote the problem on the chalkboard:

$$5 \times 5 = 25$$

"Five rows of five equal twenty-five."

2 Lore continued this activity with several drawings of squares, first showing the number of rows and columns, then filling in the rectangle as described above. The children came to the chalkboard and wrote the problem represented by each drawing.

two rows of 2
$2 \times 2 = 4$

three rows of 3
$3 \times 3 = 9$

four rows of 4
$4 \times 4 = 16$

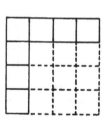

Equalities and inequalities

I
Balancing the scales

Lore used the straw scales that hang from the ceiling at one end of the room.

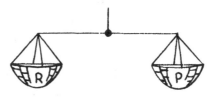

One basket is called "Red" (R) because of the red straw of the weave. The other basket is called "Purple" (P) because of the purple straw.

At the beginning of the activity, both R and P were empty. Lore asked, "Does the scale balance?" The children said yes.

1 On the chalkboard Lore drew:

"Is this true?" she asked. The children answered, "Yes."

2 Then Lore told the children to close their eyes. She put a yellow rod in P; then she told the children to open their eyes. On the chalkboard she wrote:

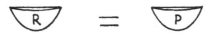

"Is this true?" she asked. A loud and resounding "No!" came from the children.

3 Lore: Suppose I did this:

Is this true?
Children: Yes.

4 The group proceeded with the game whereby the scales were balanced or not balanced depending upon whether certain rods were placed in either or in both baskets, so that the statements written on the chalkboard would vary as follows:

R > P	or	P < R
R < P	or	P > R
R = P	or	P = R
R ≠ P	or	P ≠ R

$<$, is less than; $\not<$, is not less than; $>$, is greater than; $\not>$, is not greater than; $=$, is equal to; and $\neq$, is not equal to.

II
Making true statements

Each child was given a set of 6 oaktag sheets. On each card was a different symbol. The children were to make true statements using the cards and rods as illustrated below.

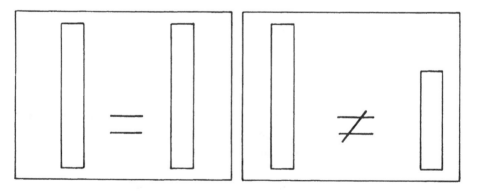

dark green equals dark green   dark green does not equal purple

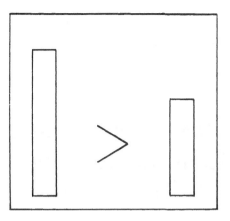

dk. gr. is greater than purple

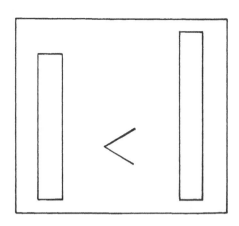

dk. gr. is smaller than black

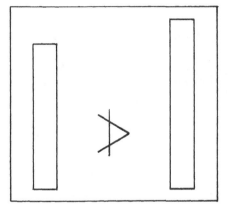

dk. gr. is not greater than black

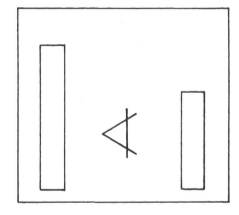

dk. gr. is not smaller than purple

Equalities and inequalities
Geometric recognition

I
Written work

The children were given lab sheets L 3 and the one diagrammed below:

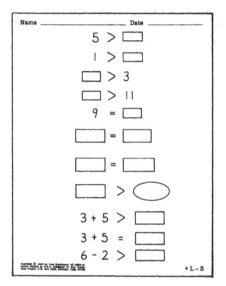

A few children occasionally used rods to determine "tricky" ways of writing a particular number, for example, $5 + 4 = 6 + 3$:

yellow (5)	purple (4)
blue (9)	
dr. green (6)	lt. gr. (3)

Eight children worked the second sheet. They had difficulty only when the box was to the left of the "equal" sign. They could work problems like these:

$$6 - 3 = \tfrac{1}{2} \times \square$$
$$4 - 2 = \tfrac{1}{2} \times \square$$

But they could not work problems like these:

$$\tfrac{1}{2} \times \square = 8 - 4$$
$$\tfrac{1}{2} \times \square = 12 - 6$$

II
Directed play with geoboards

Geoboards and rubber bands were distributed among the children.

1 Lore: Make the longest straight line you can on your geoboard.

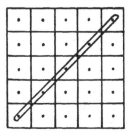

The children did this immediately.

2 Lore: Let's play "copy-cat." Copy what I make on my geoboard.

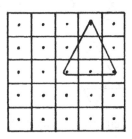

Ruthie immediately said, "It's a triangle."

3 Lore: Leave what you have on your geoboards. With another rubber band, make the same thing upside down.
The children saw that it would be a star before they had actually put the second rubber band in place.

4 Lore: What new thing do you see?
Children: A snowflake. Two triangles together.

189

5 Lore: I believe there are more triangles. Count all the triangles you see.

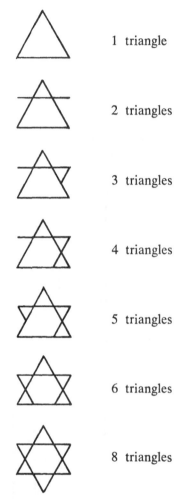

1 triangle

2 triangles

3 triangles

4 triangles

5 triangles

6 triangles

8 triangles

The children divided the middle of the star into six more triangles.

February–June

Summary of Spring Work

After January 31, the children were able to do their written work independently. They were free to select their own work from 185 lab sheets developed for them for February through June. They were also allowed to rework some of their previous lab sheets, but without using Cuisenaire® rods. None of the children worked all of the lab sheets available to them. The teacher stood by to advise and to direct activities when necessary. The children's work was incorporated into their workbooks.

Since full-group instruction was given only occasionally after January, class notes for February through June are few. A record of some of these group activities is given in the remainder of the *Diary*. These activities often lasted only about ten minutes. Most of the teacher's time was spent in preparing materials and assisting individual children.

Arithmetic operations

Children's solutions to addition problems

Lore wrote addition problems on the chalkboard and said, "I cannot get the right answer for these problems. What is an easy way of thinking to get the right answer for each problem?"

Problem: $5 + 4 = \square$

Solutions: $(5 + 5) - 1 = 10 - 1 = 9$

$(4 + 4) + 1 = 8 + 1 = 9$

Problem: $9 + 7 + 1 = \square$

Solutions: $9 + 9 = 18$, so
$9 + (7 + 2) - 1 = 9 + 9 - 1 = 18 - 1 = 17$

$(9 + 1) + 7 = 10 + 7 = 17$

Problem: $6 + 7 + 5 + 3 + 4 + 5 = \square$

Solution: $(5 + 5) + (6 + 4) + (7 + 3) = \square$
$\ 10\ \ \ + \ \ \ 10\ \ \ + \ \ \ 10\ \ = 30$

Problem:

$$12 + 13 + 12 = \square$$

Solutions:

$$(12 + 12 + 12) + 1 = 36 + 1 = 37$$
$$(12 + 12) + 10 + 3 = 24 + 10 + 3 = 37$$

Difficult problems

The following problems were written on the chalkboard and done orally by the group during several sessions. Many of the problems were selected in accordance with the types of errors the children made on lab sheets.

Multiplication:

$1 \times 1 \times 1 \times 1 \times 1 \times 1 = \square$
$364 \times 2489 \times 0 = \square$
$1 \times 1 \times 1 \times 1 \times 1 \times 1 \times 10 = \square$
$\frac{1}{2} \times \frac{1}{2} = \square$
$\frac{1}{2} \times \frac{1}{2} \times \frac{1}{2} = \square$
$\frac{1}{2} \times \frac{1}{2} \times 1 = \square$
$3 \times 3 = \square$
$6 \times \square = 0$
$9 \times \square = 18$

(Several others)

Division:

$6 \div 4 = \square$
$\square \div 3 = 4$
$\square \div 5 = 5$

Subtraction:

$\square - 4 = 3$
$\square - 5 = 1$
$\square - 3 = 6$
$\square - 7 = 4$

Correct the errors

1　Before the children came into the classroom, the teacher wrote problems on the chalkboard with correct and/or incorrect answers in the frames.

2　When the children came into the room, the teacher said: "Someone did these problems before you came in. Look at all the problems with answers. If the answer to a particular problem is *correct*, leave it on the chalkboard. If the answer is *wrong*, erase that answer from the box and place the correct answer there."

3　The following are some of the problems used in this activity:

$6 \times 3 = \boxed{15}$ *

$(3 + 2) - (2 \times 2) = \boxed{0}$ *

$9 \times 2 > \boxed{20}$ *

$3 \times 3 \times 2 = \boxed{18}$

$\boxed{2} = \tfrac{1}{2} \times (4 + 6) - (\tfrac{1}{3} \times 6)$*

$\square = 16 - 4$

$-18 < \boxed{1}$

Drill with flash cards

Flash cards were used in several group sessions during the month of April. The main purpose was to give the children practice in answering instantaneously and correctly simple problems in addition, subtraction, multiplication, and division.

Side 1 (problem)   Side 2 (answer)

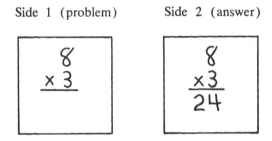

The teacher presented each problem by saying, "This is for [name of child]." Side 1 was shown to the group. When the child gave an answer, the teacher turned the flash card over so that the child saw the problem with the correct answer. If the child's answer was correct, he was given the card to keep before him on the desk. Two children could play the game by taking the parts of teacher and pupil in the same way.

Small groups of children were allowed to play the game with sets of flash cards selected in accordance with their particular needs as evidenced by their day-to-day performance in oral and written work.

Note: Surprisingly, the children loved work with the flash cards and often asked for them. No concrete materials were available for the children to use with the cards.

---

*Answers are incorrect.

Rod game

Teacher: If the *white rod* equals one, show me the rod that represents:

$\frac{1}{2} \times 10$ [Children held up the yellow rod.]
3×2 [Dark green.]
4×1 [Purple.]
$4 + 3$ [Black.]
3×3 [Blue.]
etc.

Practice in subtraction

The teacher gave the children sheets of lined paper and asked them to fold the sheets in half vertically. On the top line of one half of the sheet, the children were to write the number 20, subtract 2 mentally, and write 18. They were to continue the series, subtracting 2 each time. One side of a sheet should look like this:

20
18
16
14
12
10
 8
etc.

On the other side of the sheet, children were to write 30 and subtract 3 each time.

Note: Several children continued these series into negative numbers.

A game of Lotto

Each child was given a Lotto card.

$9 - 4$	$2 + 5$	3×4
$10 - 3$	$8 + 4$	$6 - 1$
$5 + 4$	$2 + 4$	$1 - 4$

The problems varied on each child's card.

As Lore held up a rod, the children placed the rod of the same color on each problem whose answer was represented by that color.

Number-line rules

The children dictated rules for moving along the number line; the inverse of each rule was determined by the group.

Following are some of the rules and their inverses.

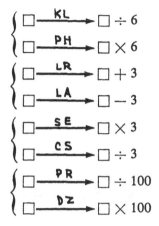

$$\left\{ \begin{array}{l} \square \xrightarrow{\text{KL}} \square \div 6 \\ \square \xrightarrow{\text{PH}} \square \times 6 \end{array} \right.$$

$$\left\{ \begin{array}{l} \square \xrightarrow{\text{LR}} \square + 3 \\ \square \xrightarrow{\text{LA}} \square - 3 \end{array} \right.$$

$$\left\{ \begin{array}{l} \square \xrightarrow{\text{SE}} \square \times 3 \\ \square \xrightarrow{\text{CS}} \square \div 3 \end{array} \right.$$

$$\left\{ \begin{array}{l} \square \xrightarrow{\text{PR}} \square \div 100 \\ \square \xrightarrow{\text{DZ}} \square \times 100 \end{array} \right.$$

The children practiced moving on the number line, using these rules and their inverses.

Division

The teacher demonstrated the problem, "How many 4's in 12?"

$$12 \div 4 = \square$$

orange (10)		red (2)
purple (4)	purple (4)	purple (4)

So, $12 \div 4 = \boxed{3}$

Practice problems

$$10 \div 2 = \square$$
$$9 \div 3 = \square$$
$$\square = 14 \div 7$$
$$8 \div 2 = \square$$
$$\bigcirc = 6 \div 6$$

The children were able to solve these problems easily whenever they read the problem, "How many 5's in 25?"

Counting

Practice in counting

Diagrams like the ones below were drawn on the chalkboard. Children counted by 2's, 3's, 5's, or 10's, as each diagram suggested.

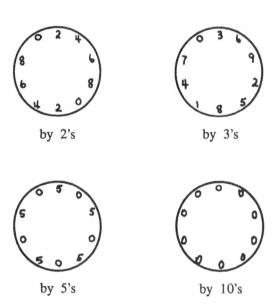

by 2's   by 3's

by 5's   by 10's

Frame arithmetic

What is the equation?

One child wrote $3 \times \square$ on the chalkboard. Then the children substituted numbers for the box and figured out answers to the problems:

$$3 \times \boxed{4}$$
$$3 \times \boxed{12}$$
$$3 \times \boxed{62}$$
$$3 \times \boxed{100}$$

One child said, "Three times nine million and nine." Lore had to write the problem and provide the answer.

Lore asked the children to make *some number larger (increase) by 5.* They wrote $5 \times \square$ and $\square \times 5$ on the chalkboard. These are incorrect. Then one child wrote $\square + 5$. This is correct.

Lore asked the children to make *eleven more than some number.* One child wrote $11 + \square$ (or, $\square + 11$). Lore asked the children to write *some number divided by 6.*

$$\square \div 6 \qquad \frac{\square}{6}$$

Chalkboard work

Problem

$$\diamondsuit + \diamondsuit = 8$$

The children knew that the "diamonds" suggested using the same number to make the equation true.

199

Problem

Question: "If we could just keep on putting numbers in the how many numbers could we use?"

The children said that there is an infinite number of possibilities.

What is the number?

Lore: I am thinking of a whole number between 0 and 100.

From questions the children asked, it was determined that:

☐ *is not* between 10 and 20.
☐ *is not* between 40 and 50.
☐ *is* between 90 and 100.
☐ is between 95 and 100.
☐ is odd.
☐ is 99.

Equalities and inequalities

Make it true, make it false

Lore wrote a problem on the chalkboard:

$$7 + 3 = 10$$

Then she asked the children to make it false without erasing anything.

$$7 + 3 \neq 10$$
$$17 + 3 = 10$$
$$7 + 3 = 100$$

Then she asked the children to make true statements without an eraser:

$$27 + 3 \neq 10$$
$$30 - (17 + 3) = 10$$
$$7 + 3 \neq 100$$

Doubling and halving

Cuisenaire® rod game

Each child was given a box of Cuisenaire® rods, all the same color.

1 Lore: Take one rod from your box and place it on the table before you. Leave that rod in place.

2 Lore: Now take from your box twice (two times) as much wood as you have before you; place that on the table and leave it there.

3 Lore: Look at your pile; now take twice as much as that and put with your pile.

4 Lore: Now add twice as many as (double) your last pile.

5 Lore: Remove half of your biggest pile. How many do you have left? Remove half. Remove half again.

The purpose of this doubling and halving activity was to get the children to discover that when we

a. double once, the result is *two times* what we started with.

$$\boxed{I} + \boxed{I} = 2$$

$$2 \times \boxed{I} = 2$$

b. double twice (double, double) the result is *four times* what we started out with.

$$\triangle{2} + \triangle{2} = 4$$

$$4 \times \boxed{I} = 4$$

c. double three times (double, double, double) the result is *eight times* what we started with.

$$\textcircled{4} + \textcircled{4} = 8$$

$$8 \times \boxed{I} = 8$$

We can *undo* what was accomplished through the doubling activity by *halving*.

$$\tfrac{1}{2} \times 8 = 4$$
$$\tfrac{1}{2} \times 4 = 2$$
$$\tfrac{1}{2} \times 2 = 1$$

6 Lore: Find two rods of the *same color* that will be as much wood as I am holding up."

black
yellow

Children held up

dark green
dark green

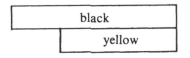

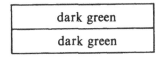

7 Lore held up several other combinations:

yellow and light green [The children held up 2 purple rods]

black and light green [2 yellow]

orange and purple [2 black]

Fractions

Work with Cuisenaire® rods

Each child was given a paper plate, and a box of Cuisenaire® rods was placed on each table.

1 Lore: Place in your plate *one black rod* and one white rod. (Note: rods were described by color name, not a number name.)

2 Lore: If the black rod equals 1, what is the white rod?
Danny: One-seventh of 1.

3 Lore: Take a red rod. If the white rod is called $\frac{1}{7}$ what is the red one called?
Bobby: $\frac{2}{7}$

4 What is the yellow rod called?
Jeff: $\frac{5}{7}$

5 Lore wrote this problem on the chalkboard: $\frac{5}{7} + \frac{1}{7} = \square$
Lore: What rod would we call $\frac{6}{7}$?
Child: Dark green.

6 Lore: These are called *fractions*. [She wrote the word on the chalkboard.]

7 Lore: Here is a problem for you. Place your dark green rod end to end with your yellow rod. How shall I write the problem?
The children dictated the problem:
$$\frac{6}{7} + \frac{5}{7} = \square$$

8 Lore: What is another name for $\frac{11}{7}$?

The children were puzzled.

Lore: How many 1's are there in $\frac{11}{7}$?

Child: One 1 in $\frac{11}{7}$.

Lore: And what is left over (how many $\frac{1}{7}$'s?)

Children: Four $\frac{1}{7}$'s.

Lore demonstrated this with rods.

one black + four whites

$1 \quad + \frac{4}{7}$ or $1\frac{4}{7}$

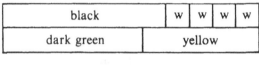

$\frac{6}{7} + \frac{5}{7} = \frac{11}{7}$ or $1\frac{4}{7}$

one dark green + yellow

The children then dictated the following problems and gave answers:

Problem	Answer
$\frac{6}{7} - \frac{5}{7} = \square$	$\frac{1}{7}$
$\frac{10}{7} - \frac{8}{7} = \square$	$\frac{2}{7}$
$1\frac{3}{7} - \frac{5}{7} = \square$	$\frac{5}{7}$

The children had no difficulty with the problem:

$$1\frac{3}{7} - \frac{5}{7} = \square$$

Lore asked "how many sevenths in 1?" Children said seven $\frac{1}{7}$'s. Then,

$$\frac{7}{7} + \frac{3}{7} = \frac{10}{7}$$

and

$$\frac{10}{7} - \frac{5}{7} = \frac{5}{7}$$

Comment: There might have been more experiences like the one described. The children were ready for this work.

Word problems

School event problems

The children were asked the prices of various items at the Miquon Fair.

Ferris wheel	20¢
hamburger	30¢
pony ride	25¢
jeep ride	25¢
kitten	$1.00
hot dog	25¢
turtle	30¢
clown	25¢
fishing	10¢
puppet show	25¢
hayride	25¢
pop	10¢
recorder	$1.00

The following are word problems that Lore and the children constructed orally in a group session.

A boy bought 2 hamburgers and 1 pop. How much did he spend?

8 pony rides and 2 Ferris wheel rides cost _____?

A boy's mother gave him half a dollar. He bought a hot dog and a soda pop. How much change did he get?

A girl bought 2 turtles, 3 jeep rides and a recorder. How much money did she spend?

A boy was at the fair without his mother. She told him that he could buy one thing each. How much money did he spend?

Time

Lore drew a diagram of a clock on the chalkboard:

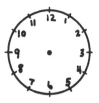

1 Lore: I had to go to Harrisburg yesterday. I was supposed to be there at this time: 9:15 A.M. [chalkboard]. Who will read this time to me (as indicated on the chalkboard)?

Children: Nine fifteen A.M.; fifteen after nine; quarter after nine.

Now come to the chalkboard and draw a picture of the hands on the diagram of the clock.

A child came forward and drew in the hands correctly.

2 Lore: From one numeral to the next (on the clock) is 5 minutes. So we can count five (1), ten (2), fifteen (3), etc., etc. .... sixty (12), the next hour.

3 Lore: I had to be in Harrisburg at 9:15 A.M.; so I checked the train schedule. The first train I could catch was scheduled to arrive in Harrisburg at 9:45 A.M. Was this a good time for me to arrive in Harrisburg (if I was to be there at 9:15)?

Children: No! 9:45 is after 9:15. You'd be late.

4 Lore: Change the picture (diagram of clock) to indicate 9:45 A.M. Use another color chalk. [One child responded correctly.]

5 Lore: How late would I have been had I taken that train?

The children made guesses of 25 minutes and 30 minutes. The children proved their last answer by counting on the diagram of the clock.

6 Lore: This is the time I actually arrived in Harrisburg:

Children: You got there at 9:00.
Lore: Was I early or was I late?
Children: You were 15 minutes early.

7 Lore: Don drove me to Harrisburg and Stevie and Frankie went with us. We got up at 6:10 A.M. [on chalkboard]. Who can read what is written on the chalkboard?
Children: Ten minutes after six.
"We must leave," Don said, "no later than 7:00 A.M., even if you haven't had your breakfast." How many minutes did we have from 6:10 to 7:00 to wash, brush our teeth, get dressed, and eat breakfast before it was time to leave?
Children: 50 minutes (counting by fives on diagram).

8 Lore: Frankie was there at 6:53 A.M. How many minutes before the time we were supposed to leave was Frankie there?
Children: 7 minutes.
Lore: We didn't leave at seven o'clock, though. Know why? Don was not ready. It was chilly and he had to go back into the house to get his jacket.
We did not leave our house until 7:12 A.M. We arrived at the gate of the turnpike at 7:15 A.M.
Child: You must live awfully close to the turnpike if it took only 3 minutes for you to get there.

9 Lore: We were at the turnpike gate at 7:15 A.M. and we arrived in Harrisburg at 9:00 A.M. How long did it take us to get there?
Child: One and three-quarter hours.
Lore: How do you write that?
The child wrote $1\frac{3}{4}$ hr. and 1 hr. 45 min.

10 Lore: How many minutes is that?
Children: 105 minutes. [They added 60 minutes and 45 minutes.]
Louis: How fast did you travel?
Lore wrote on the chalkboard
      Lore's house to Harrisburg $\approx$ 100 miles
(She explained that this new symbol means "about" or "approximately.")

11 Lore: If we went 100 miles in 105 minutes, how fast did we travel?

Child: 60 miles per hour.

This story could have been stretched out a little longer, but one of the children noticed the clock. It was five minutes after 12 o'clock noon: time for lunch.

Number of written problems solved by first-graders

Numerator—correctly solved problems
Denominator—problems done

Anne	$\frac{2000}{2100}$	Ruthie	$\frac{1000}{1130}$
David G.	$\frac{1900}{2000}$	Gary	$\frac{1000}{1050}$
David C.	$\frac{1750}{1950}$	Ben	$\frac{910}{1010}$
Danny B.	$\frac{1700}{1820}$	Eric	$\frac{850}{1000}$
Louis	$\frac{1450}{1600}$	Rodney	$\frac{850}{930}$
Audrey	$\frac{1300}{1500}$	*David T.	$\frac{561}{708}$
Fred	$\frac{1250}{1400}$	*Andrea	$\frac{383}{487}$
Jeff	$\frac{1210}{1350}$	*Peter R.	$\frac{425}{485}$
Danny S.	$\frac{1100}{1300}$		
Lynn	$\frac{1180}{1300}$		
Peter H.	$\frac{1080}{1250}$		
Bobby H.	$\frac{1030}{1200}$		

*Indicates that child entered in the middle of the year.

Index

This index is intended as a guide to the learning activities chronicled in the *First-Grade Diary* for the year 1960-61 at the Miquon School. It is arranged in thirteen topics, each broken down chronologically with the day's activity listed. The index does not attempt to list every mention of every topic. For example, under the heading "Fractions" the reader will find the activities and written work that deal *extensively* with fractions, but he will not find every mention of a problem involving fractions.

Nor does the index include the arithmetic operations, addition, subtraction, multiplication, and division, since these occur in most activities throughout the school year. The operations generally are named, where appropriate, in headings under the date in the text.

The reader will notice that the topics "Cuisenaire® rods" and "Number line" are included in the index. Since these are the two most important concrete materials used with the Math Lab Materials and are ones with which the teacher may be unfamiliar, the index provides a comprehensive guide to their many uses.

213